RECOVERY FROM COMPULSIVE BEHAVIOR

How To Transcend Your Troubled Family

Lane Lasater, Ph.D.

Illustrations By Janet E. Gustafson
Foreword By Sharon Wegscheider-Cruse

Health Communications, Inc.
Deerfield Beach, Florida

Lane Lasater
Boulder, Colorado

Library of Congress Cataloging-in-Publication Data
Lasater, Lane.
  Recovery from compulsive behavior.

  1. Compulsive behavior. I. Title.
RC 533.L27   616.85'227   88-9326

Published by Health Communications, Inc.
                Enterprise Center
                3201 Southwest 15th Street
                Deerfield Beach, FL 33442

FOREWORD

I have known Lane Lasater for several years and have been privileged to be a part of his recovery process. Lane has also worked with me as a facilitator in my Family Reconstruction Workshops. He is a skilled and empathic therapist who is clear in his own recovery. That clarity shows in *Recovery From Compulsive Behavior*.

A short time ago, information about co-dependency was in short supply. In the last year or two, however, we have been deluged with an abundance of books, tapes and films dealing with co-dependency. We have moved from a problem of supply to one of selection. The time has come to develop discernment and select recovery materials best suited for us.

I would select *Recovery From Compulsive Behavior*. It offers clarity about the illness of co-dependency and hope that co-dependency is treatable. And it provides tools for recovery. The brief self-assessment questionnaires throughout the book are valuable, easy-to-use aids to self-understanding. They are helpful in identifying recovery issues for individuals. They are also tools professionals can use in working with clients.

Because Lane has traveled the path he teaches, his guidelines for changing compulsive behavior are practical and workable. The images for recovery, from "Hitting the Rapids" to "Dancing through the Rattlesnakes," are vivid illustrations of various steps in recovery and pitfalls along the way. My own favorite is "The Mother Lion," which was literally created in a dream when Lane was a facilitator at one of my workshops. It is a reminder of his power and creativity as a therapist.

Lane shares that creativity in *Recovery From Compulsive Behavior*. It is a valuable addition to the available information about co-dependency.

Sharon Wegscheider-Cruse
President
Onsite Training and Consulting, Inc.

ACKNOWLEDGMENTS

This book would not have been possible without the great faith, patience, encouragement and constructive criticism of my wife and partner, Nancy B. Larson Lasater. I want to thank my sons, Colin and Jonathan, for continually reminding me of the preciousness and importance of childhood. I thank Dr. Peter Ossorio for his friendship and inspiration throughout my career, for teaching me the principles of Descriptive Psychology, helping me conceptualize the book and originating the use of images in psychotherapy. I thank Janet Gustafson for bringing the images for recovery to life so beautifully. It has been a joy to work with her. Certain people have made great contributions to the book along the way: Laurie Lasater and Annette Nixon Lasater guided me throughout toward making the book straightforward and accessible; Bob Wells served as a valuable critic and overall manager, keeping his standards high and connecting me with resources along the way; Dan Mason urged me to put myself into the book and made helpful editorial changes; and Leslie Burger did a beautiful job of editing as the book neared completion. Sharon Wegscheider-Cruse, Dr. Joseph Cruse, Mary Roush, Verna Salmon, Helice Fox, Dr. Claudia Black, Dr. Gary Forrest and Jack Kerner gave me encouragement to keep going when I really needed it. Jim Larson, David Silburn, Dale Lasater, Sally Lasater, Dr. Tim Stokes, Susan Morgan, Dr. Barry Schreiber and Kate Fotopolous all read early manuscripts and made helpful suggestions. Cecelia

Maxwell suggested the "His Dream/Her Dream" image and Sophie Morgan suggested the "Dancing Through the Rattlesnakes" image. Dr. Carolyn Zeiger, Shelley Stuart-Bullock and Linda Reed suggested important improvements on the images. I thank you all!

DEDICATION

This book is dedicated to my mother and father.

CONTENTS

INTRODUCTION

After volleyball and a cookout, a group of us sat drinking wine and talking, enjoying the cool summer evening. This good-bye party marked the end of my three-month training experience at the Five County Human Development Center in central Minnesota. Over the past year, during my clinical psychology internship at the University of Minnesota Health Sciences Center, I had discovered how fascinating it was to understand whole human lives. I had seen how each person's development continued throughout the unique circumstances of his or her life. I was thrilled to be in this field. In a few days I would start a one-year fellowship in child, adolescent and family psychology in Minneapolis. When I finished writing my doctoral dissertation, my graduate training would be complete.

I liked and respected this group of mental health professionals. They worked with difficult families that were troubled with alcoholism, child abuse and violence. During my summer at their clinic, they had taught me about being genuine and loving. Their personal wisdom, developed from broad life experiences, gave them special compassion for people and families in pain. I wanted to become that kind of helper.

As the evening went on, I kept drinking wine. We started talking about our families. To be funny, I told about a time at age 11 when I had unsuccessfully tried to stop my parents' violent argument. I laughed about my ineffectiveness as a family therapist.

My friends greeted my story with silence. I regretted opening my mouth because I had revealed that my family was troubled and that I was emotionally unfinished with the past. For a long time, I had kept secret my feeling of shame about my troubled childhood and my fear that I was emotionally unworthy of my profession. Up to that moment I had considered my training almost complete. Over the next few months, it became apparent that the last and most important dimension of my preparation as a helper was only beginning. Now I needed to heal myself.

During the weeks after the party, I struggled to come to terms with my feelings about the past. I finally decided that I needed professional help and called a therapist recommended by my supervisor. At our first meeting, he asked me many questions about my family life as I was growing up. He was also interested in my drinking. During the second session, he informed me that he thought I was in trouble with alcohol and recommended that I stop drinking. Even though I knew he was right, my heart sank. Alcohol gave me breaks from life and seemed to help me cope with the challenges of adulthood.

I realized that I had been an alcoholic from my earliest drinking experiences. I thought that one was supposed to drink to get drunk. I blacked out the first time I drank, at age 18, and many times thereafter. I had struggled for years to drink in a controlled way. Now the secret was out.

I haven't had a drink since that day. My therapist introduced me to recovering alcoholics who showed me the possibilities of life without alcohol. During my months of early sobriety, he helped me begin to discover my feelings and start my process of emotional healing from childhood. I did not realize it then, but I had many miles to go in recovery. Over the next few years I was fortunate to have therapists and teachers and friends who helped me transform my life.

There have been several stages to my recovery. First, I had to remove the anesthetic of alcohol so that I could begin to feel again. Next, I had to stop creating professional conflicts by my unsuccessful attempts to reform organizations and bureaucracies where I worked. I also had to stop trying to change my parents. Over the years of recovery, I had to eventually stop my cigarette smoking and compulsive overeating and working and learn to take care of myself.

As I reduced the compulsive behavior in my life, I recognized feelings of grief, anger, hurt and shame connected to childhood experiences. My family experience during childhood was a combination of pain and joy. There was great love in my family, but terrible conflict and hurt as well. I realized that I became a helper as a little boy, trying to make things better in my family. When I was unable to help them, I became angry. I rebelled against my parents, and our bitter conflicts tried them greatly. I also turned my anger against myself. By the time I reached drinking age, I was already in great emotional pain.

In spite of the pain, there were many wonderful moments in my childhood. My parents were cattle ranchers and the whole family worked together each summer. My father spent many days teaching my brothers, my sister and me how to raise and care for animals and to respect nature and the environment. My mother loved people. She showed me great tenderness and taught me how to be gentle and caring to others. Both my parents believed in education and helped me with mine. The wisdom that my parents taught me has greatly benefited me through the years as I have cared for others.

As my recovery progressed, the negative things that had happened in my life ceased to dominate me emotionally. I came to understand that what happened in my family resulted from several generations of unfinished emotional business. I saw that my parents, too, were trapped, and I recognized their suffering. I learned to appreciate my life as it was, realizing that I became a more compassionate person because of my childhood struggles. I no longer felt resentful about the past. Through personal recovery and professional experience, I now understand that troubled behavior and emotional patterns can be transformed into strength and wisdom. In this book, I offer you what I have learned.

1. DO COMPULSIVE PATTERNS AFFECT YOU?

We live in an age of compulsive behavior. Many of us are locked into habits and emotions that we feel powerless to change. Repetitive behavior patterns diminish the quality of our lives as we find ourselves employing the same ineffective, even destructive, strategies over and over, almost unwillingly.

For example, we may find ourselves working 70 hours a week to advance a career while living in an emotional vacuum at home or going overboard in an effort to create a perfect, "loving" relationship that never seems to come into being. Some of us are always struggling with people and organizations that don't do things the way we think they should. Or we repeatedly make career or relationship decisions that are not in our best interests. Some of us just don't want to grow up and face adult responsibility.

Many of us don't respect ourselves, or we struggle with anxiety or depression. We find it hard to build relationships that work. We encounter setbacks in life that we did not expect, or we feel great pressure to compete for survival. Escapes are available on all sides. We may turn to alcohol, drugs, cigarettes, food, sexual affairs or other ways to soften the edge of life. Before we know it, our escapes have taken over our lives.

1

Our problem emotions and behavior began to evolve during our childhood, as we adapted to troubled families and environments. Each of our families passed on to us a unique set of strengths and limitations — resources that may or may not have prepared us for adult life. Our childhood strategies for survival may have led us into later compulsive patterns. These patterns begin subtly and sneak up on us. They represent an accumulation of choices that were made one at a time, choices that seemed right at the time but ultimately didn't work out. Such choices were made without clear awareness.

We can begin to make the changes needed to interrupt these patterns in *recovery*, which involves understanding our childhood strategies, healing from the hurts of the past and finding new, constructive ways of living. We can overcome our problem emotions and resolve the childhood fears that underlie them. By facing negative patterns in our lives, we can transcend our troubled families and arrive at levels of satisfaction that we have never reached before. We can reduce the chronic distress in our lives and invest our energy in more rewarding pursuits.

This book is an invitation to undertake an expedition in personal growth. The journey from compulsive behavior patterns to emotional and behavioral freedom is difficult, and most of us are not able to do it on our own. We need a map and a guide who knows the territory. We need to prepare, plan, study, train and persevere. There will be more twists and turns than we can anticipate. But we can make it!

If this book can help you understand your problem behavior more quickly and clearly than you might otherwise, then it will have served its purpose. If it can help you make the changes that you desire, then you can avoid some of the needless suffering that is the result of all compulsive behavior.

The book provides a map to follow as you explore your strengths and vulnerabilities and make the changes you want in your life. It offers you:

1. An explanation of how adults develop common problem emotional and behavior patterns
2. Specific instructions and tools to use in moving from problem patterns to emotional and behavioral freedom

3. Descriptions of people who have recovered from these patterns
4. Visual images or metaphors to accompany central ideas in this book

You Can Overcome Problem Patterns

You may be wondering, "Do I have what it takes to overcome my problem patterns?" The answer is yes! Moving from repetitive patterns to behavioral and emotional freedom requires a gradual change in your attitudes and behavior. Making positive choices requires that you clearly understand the problems you face and set priorities in relation to them. This book gives you a framework for understanding your problem behavior and establishing personal priorities. Positive change requires only that you put forth the effort you are capable of, one day at a time.

You are already engaged in this change process because you are reading this book. Give yourself the credit you deserve for the effort you are making. You will find that you *do* have the ability to overcome problems, outgrow old patterns and transform your life.

Three Kinds Of Adult Problems

This book deals with three varieties of adult emotional and behavioral problems: *problem emotional adjustments,* which begin in childhood; and two forms of compulsive behavior, *compulsive life patterns* and *compulsive escapes.* We now understand childhood adjustments and compulsive behavior patterns very clearly because of developments in the study of addiction and the fields of family therapy and psychotherapy. Pioneers in alcoholic family theory, such as Sharon Wegscheider-Cruse, Claudia Black, Robert Ackerman and Janet Woititz, have helped create national awareness of families affected by alcohol abuse. The term *co-dependency* was coined originally to describe the compulsive feelings and behavior of spouses of alcoholics. Now we know that families affected by alcohol problems often represent extremes of these patterns, but the principles of compulsive behavior apply to some degree to most troubled families. This book describes how compulsive patterns develop and how they can be changed.

Problem Emotional Adjustments

Problem emotional adjustments start as we adapt to childhood environments that significantly limit our choices. We frequently bring these problem adjustments with us into adulthood, long after the need for them — survival — exists. Our self-perception, world view and means of protecting ourselves remain the same as when we were children. As a result, we maintain or unwittingly re-create the limitations of our childhood environment as we move into adult life. Common problem emotional adjustments are:

1. Low self-esteem
2. Unresolved emotions
3. Difficulty trusting

Compulsive Life Patterns

Our childhood strategies and problem emotional adjustments often lead to compulsive behavior patterns in adulthood. Compulsive patterns are characterized by an inability to stop certain ways of acting even when these no longer serve our best interests. These patterns are widespread in modern society. There are five compulsive life patterns common among adults.

1. **Compulsive working** is working or thinking about work excessively.
2. **Relationship dependency** is investing time, energy and affection in people who do not reciprocate what we offer them.
3. **Generalized rebellion** is engaging in frequent conflicts with organizations or troubled people.
4. **Victim syndrome** means participating naively or passively in decisions that affect our well-being.
5. **Perpetual-child syndrome** means not following through on commitments or taking adult responsibility in our lives.

Compulsive Escapes

Our problem emotional adjustments and compulsive life patterns create pain, which often leads us to seek escapes that can become compulsive:

1. Alcohol, drug and cigarette abuse
2. Over- and undereating
3. Compulsive sexual behavior
4. Compulsive spending
5. Compulsive religious behavior
6. Compulsive gambling
7. Compulsive exercising

Changing Our Lives

Most of us are troubled to some degree by problem emotional adjustments, compulsive life patterns and compulsive escapes. Richard's life illustrates how one person struggled with and overcame low self-esteem, unresolved emotions, relationship dependency and compulsive overeating during recovery.

Richard's Parenting Crisis

Richard trembled visibly as he recalled a confrontation with his son, Scott, the previous night. "Scott came home very late, and when I asked him about this, he swore at me. I lost it and almost slugged him." Richard was shocked by the intensity of his anger. He wanted to understand his out-of-control feelings before he did something he would regret.

The Roots Of Richard's Compulsion

As Richard was growing up, his parents constantly fought about his father's compulsive working. Richard was lonely and felt unaccepted by his father. He was given a lot of responsibility for his younger brothers. He tried to counsel his parents to create a happy family situation, but his efforts to help failed. He came out of childhood feeling unwanted and unworthy as a son.

From childhood, Richard's low self-esteem, loneliness and frustration led him to comfort and console himself with food.

His overeating became a compulsive escape pattern, and now, as an adult, he was considerably overweight.

Richard married a woman who was irresponsible and not prepared for the commitment of marriage and raising a child. This choice forced him to take over most of the responsibility in the family and started a pattern of relationship dependency. The marriage failed, and he was left alone with responsibility for his son.

After the divorce, Richard devoted a great deal of energy to taking care of his son. He wanted to give Scott all of the opportunities he had missed during his own childhood. Scott's rebellion threatened Richard's wish to have a child he could be proud of. Richard's attempts to control Scott only hardened this teenager's normal quest for autonomy.

Richard's Recovery Tasks

"I can't control Scott. I am afraid I am going to lose him." To release Scott and to allow him to take responsibility for his own choices, Richard had to face the unresolved grief and anger from his own childhood. As he healed from his childhood pain, Richard gradually ceased his struggle to control his son, and Scott no longer needed to push him away so forcefully. Richard began to value and care for himself directly. As part of his self-care, he changed his eating patterns and began to lose his extra weight. For the first time in his life, he began to consciously plan ways to fulfill himself that went beyond his commitment to parenting.

Stages Of Behavior Change

We go through six stages as we change ourselves. Remember these as you learn about and change your problem behavior patterns.

1. **Recognition** happens when we see that a certain problem or set of problems belongs to us.
2. **Hope** develops when we become aware that other people have had these problems and have overcome them.
3. **Clarity** develops as we understand how these problems developed and why they continue.

4. **Preparation** involves gathering the strength to come to terms with the losses, changes and effort involved in carrying out these changes.
5. **Action** continues over a long period of time and in small increments. It begins as we self-consciously stop our old behavior and practice new patterns of action.
6. **Continuation** means managing our lives so that we can carry on our positive behavior and avoid creating new problems.

This book is designed to assist you in moving through these stages of behavior change. Chapter 2 discusses how the strengths and stresses of our childhood environments provided the foundations for adult behavior patterns. Chapter 3 describes common ways that we adapted as children to limitations in our families. Chapters 4, 5 and 6 describe problem emotional adjustments, compulsive life patterns and compulsive escapes. These chapters help you achieve *recognition, hope* and *clarity*. Chapters 7 and 8 describe the many recovery resources we now have available, identify tasks for recovery and focus on *preparation* for recovery. Chapters 9, 10 and 11 present tools for recovery *action* and *continuation* of the growth we have achieved.

Image 1 provides you with a reminder about the sometimes desperate reality of our compulsive behavior patterns. Most of us wait until we are sure that our old ways of doing things are not working before we try something else. We may have waited to address our problem emotional and behavioral patterns until a crisis has developed. The image portrays that moment of crisis (p. 8).

Hitting the Rapids. *Our compulsive behavior patterns are represented by this canoe on the verge of sinking in raging rapids. At one time the canoe was a faithful tool, but now it has become a trap. The negative consequences of compulsive behavior were manageable once, but now they have become a torrent. Information and support from others, which we need to overcome compulsive behavior patterns, are represented by the life ring. In order to reach the ring, we must abandon the waning security of the canoe and leap to the life ring. This means coming to terms with painful reality and facing powerful emotions. But through the leap, we can receive the help of others and reach the shore. Good luck on your leap!*

2. OUR CHILDHOOD FOUNDATION

Just what does our early child-hood environment have to do with our current problems? How do we evaluate our childhood family environment? What other childhood influences make a difference in our development? This chapter lets you assess your family's strengths and the limitations you faced during childhood as you begin to understand the origins of your adult behavior patterns.

The Importance Of Family Learning

The family is our first learning context. We observe our parents' actions and model their behavior. As we develop, we learn directly and indirectly from other family members about ourselves, others and the world, and about how to be a good family member. We receive messages such as "Don't expect too much," "I love you," "Wait your turn," "You are a good girl," "That's not good enough," "Get a good education," "It's okay to make mistakes," "Don't bother me," and "I'm glad you are here."

Even siblings may have been exposed to varying family environments because of changes in family finances, changes in our parents' relationship, the departure of older siblings or the presence of grandparents or other relatives. Often we did not have opportunities to closely observe families different from our own; thus, we took for granted that the way things were in our family was how things were in the world. In families where problems predominated over family strengths, we instinctively learned that our goal was to survive.

Through the family education process, we developed *skills*, including *knowledge, values, abilities* and *beliefs* about ourselves and the world. Coping with troubled family systems required that we emphasize certain skills and de-emphasize others, so that we become good at those we practiced most often. Our particular patterns of skills and *deficits* prepared us accordingly for success in situations that we faced later. The more skills we developed, the more choices were available to us, and the more enhanced our lives became.

Your family may have provided an environment rich in opportunity for constructive emotional expression, yet lacking in encouragement for intellectual curiosity and development. On the other hand, you may have found it necessary to take on responsibility beyond your years in order to survive. Unfortunately, due to an unsupportive emotional environment and your lack of preparation, you may have been unable to take credit for that ability and consequently developed little self-confidence. You may have learned that adults relax and have fun by drinking alcohol, or that working on hobbies is fun or that adults never have fun because they always work.

Basic Human Needs

The best way to understand our requirements for family environments is in terms of basic human needs, a concept introduced by Abraham Maslow (1943). My research shows that we experience well-being when we live in an environment that allows us to meet the following ten basic human needs to a reasonable degree (1983):

1. Physical health
2. Safety and security
3. Love and affection
4. Self-esteem
5. Belonging
6. Autonomy

7. Predictability and legitimacy
8. Recreation
9. Identity
10. Meaning and hope

Most of these needs are self-explanatory; *legitimacy* means having human rights and receiving fair and just treatment, and *identity* means defining and knowing our personal strengths, limitations, philosophy and morality. When our basic human needs are frustrated, we experience fear, anger, sadness, grief or guilt. As frustration continues, we often develop compulsive behavior patterns as misguided attempts to meet our basic human needs. If our needs are frustrated for extended periods of time, we develop stress disorders, frequent illness and ultimately chronic disorders such as heart disease, cancer or arthritis.

Your Basic Human Needs

Were you able to meet your basic human needs during childhood? Are you able to meet your basic human needs now? Using the following scale, rate the truth of each statement for you during childhood and now. Use a 2-10 scale as follows: 2 = very untrue of me, 4 = moderately untrue of me, 6 = slightly true of me, 8 = moderately true of me and 10 = very true of me.

Need	Childhood	Now
1. I have good physical health.	10	4
2. I feel safe and secure.	4	4
3. I am loved by the people close to me.	8	4
4. I receive the affection I need from others.	6	2
5. I feel like I am a good and valuable person.	6	2
6. I feel comfortable and natural with important people in my life.	2	2
7. I can improve my life through my own efforts if I wish.	2	2
8. What I want is important to the people around me.	2	2
9. My life is predictable so that I can plan ahead with confidence.	2	2
10. I understand myself well.	2	2

11. I know what is natural and right for me. _2 2_

12. I do some enjoyable things just because I want to. _6 2_

13. I can relax and forget about my problems at times. _6 2_

14. What I do today will make life better for me in the future. _4 2_

15. I am hopeful that I can have the kind of life I want. _2 2_

Total _64 36_

Your Scores

Possible scores for each category (childhood and now) range from 30 to 150. Scores in the range of 30-60 indicate that you may have endured or currently endure severe need frustration. Scores in the 60-90 range suggest moderate need frustration. Scores in the 90-120 range suggest moderate need satisfaction. Scores of 120-150 suggest that your needs were or are well satisfied.

If your childhood scores fall in the range of moderate or severe need frustration, this suggests that you grew up in an environment with inadequate resources for you. If this was the case, you may want to seek a lot of support for yourself during recovery through resources such as self-help groups, psychotherapy, close friends, and church and community groups. Your answers to these questions also reveal which needs you were or are most and least able to satisfy. You can make those unmet needs a conscious priority. You can give back to yourself in recovery those things that you missed along the way.

Understanding Our Family Environments

Why were so many of us unable to meet our basic human needs in our families of childhood? We are now discovering that family troubles pass from generation to generation when children adapt to the limitations of their parents, and then as adults unknowingly convey those or other limitations to their own children. In this book, we focus on the problem emotional adjustments and compulsive behavior patterns that significantly limit our ability to parent the next generation. As adult children from troubled families, we have the responsibility to attain not just physical independence from our families of childhood but behavioral and emotional freedom from childhood limitations as well.

Relatively few families are either totally troubled or totally healthy. If we imagine family adjustment in a normal bell-shaped distribution, the midpoint would represent families with both moderate strengths and moderate problems. About 64 percent of families might fall into this middle range. Approximately 18 percent of families would be assumed to be very troubled, and approximately 18 percent would be expected to have exceptional resources and health.

Family Health

Families that enhance children's abilities to meet their basic human needs provide protection, affection, stability, support, respect, appropriate freedom and education to their members. Several characteristics are particularly important sources of family health (Curran, 1983):

1. The parents love each other and their children.
2. Family members talk and listen to each other.
3. Family members respect and support each other.
4. Family members trust and rely on each other.
5. Responsibility is shared reasonably and fairly.
6. Family members do things together as a family.
7. There are clear family values about right and wrong.
8. There are established family traditions and rituals.

Exceptional Family Health: The Stewarts

Mary and Paul Stewart spend a few minutes alone with each other before dinner every evening. They have been married 24 years but seem to maintain a romantic excitement about each other. They carefully listen to each other and to their five children. Paul and Mary often hug and kiss or have their arms around each other, and Paul usually calls Mary "sweetheart." Many children of all ages from the neighborhood frequently visit their house to play with the Stewart children. This family seems to have love to spare. Their children use the house as a home base for their various activities, and there are many comings and goings, but peace prevails.

The Stewarts are not without problems. Barney, their third child, had leukemia and died at age 12. During his illness the whole family included and supported him within the group, but each child continued to receive attention. At the time of his death, the Stewarts grieved both together and individually. They remember him at special times of the year and visit his grave together. Both Paul and Mary have strong religious faith, and this helped them face Barney's death. They belong to different churches but have accepted this difference in one another peacefully.

Some of the children do well in school and others not so well, but each member seems to have his or her own special distinction in the family for acrobatics, singing, humor, schoolwork or outdoorsmanship. The Stewarts take a summer trip together each year to a national park or wilderness campground. Everyone pitches in willingly to accomplish the camping tasks of each day. Family members seem to love being who they are individually, and they all love being "Stewarts."

Family Troubles

Our troubled families, which barely met our basic human needs, were often characterized by insecurity, distrust, volatility, criticism, conflict and distance. Our families varied greatly, however, as to whether family problems were apparent on the surface. Covert family troubles were quite damaging because we did not have dramatic external events to explain our feelings of distress. Some or all of the following characteristics were often present in the troubled family environments that gave rise to our adult problem behaviors (Norwood, 1985; and Whitfield, 1987).

1. Relationships were unpredictable and contradictory. Relationships in our troubled families often varied dramatically between friendliness and hostility. This included relationships between parents, between parents and children, and between siblings. As children in such families, we found ourselves unable to anticipate or understand sudden and dramatic shifts in behavior and mood. This situation undermined our security and our ability to trust others.

Caught In The Middle

Alice could not rely on being close to either of her parents for long. Because she reminded her mother of herself as a girl, her mother was sometimes very close and inviting and sometimes critical and cold toward Alice. Her mother had a particularly hard time supporting Alice as a young teenager, when Alice was vulnerable and needed compassion. In addition, her mother resented her husband's affection for Alice, and Alice felt that she had to conceal her affection for her father. He would then pull back, and she often felt doubly abandoned.

2. Children were given adult responsibility. Many times in our troubled families we felt assigned to or pulled into adult roles (Bowen, 1976). As children we lacked the maturity, knowledge and experience to assume emotional or practical responsibility for other family members, especially parents. Yet, if we perceived that a parent or both parents needed our help, we would often try to make things better by trying to counsel the adults or becoming an emotional surrogate husband or wife. No matter how well we may have carried out our "adult" responsibilities at the time, we often came away with powerful feelings of inadequacy as adults. In addition, we interrupted our normal developmental tasks.

Trying To Fill His Father's Place

Hugh's father was away a great deal pursuing his career, and Hugh, as the eldest son, was pulled into being an emotional confidant for his mother. She turned to him to make up for the lack of support and intimacy that she felt in her marriage. As a result of their closeness, Hugh's mother made allowances for his school failures and irresponsible spending. He failed to learn to take full responsibility for himself, and his father was extremely critical about this. Hugh felt rejected, and he couldn't accept his father even though he needed his father's guidance and modeling.

3. Affection and supervision were inappropriate. Frequently, like Hugh, we received too much affection and protection, with the result that we were smothered and inhibited from developing our own autonomy and responsibility. Or we received too little affection and supervision and as a result felt unloved and emotionally deprived. Extreme styles of affection sometimes coexisted within the same parent or parent figure. A parent or older sibling would be very affectionate one moment and harsh and rigid the next. This inconsistency created an unpredictable and unmanageable childhood environment.

Rejected As A Person

Ginny, an adopted child, felt she was treated as an object rather than as a person. When her actions and behavior pleased her mother, her mother would be very affectionate, but when Ginny went against her mother's authority, she would be rejected coldly and reminded that she was fortunate to be living in this family. Ginny felt that her role was that of a showpiece rather than as a unique and valuable person. She carried her deep loneliness and need for affection into adulthood. She felt that her relationships were doomed because she always tried to find a man who could make up for the love she had missed.

4. We were emotionally isolated in our families. Claudia Black (1981) points out that many families have an implicit rule that family matters are not to be talked about, either with family members or with people outside the family. The net result was often emotional isolation for us as children. We became very guarded in talking to people outside our families because there was a great deal that we could not talk about. Our isolation and distrust often remain with us later in life.

Family Secrets

Kevin's family had a reputation as a "super family" in his community. The children were highly visible and recognized for both academic and athletic accomplishments. Their home life was a different story, with his mother drinking and his father at times suicidal. These family "secrets" were not acknowledged because Kevin's father viewed them as evidence of weakness, which he could not accept. More secrets were added as the years went on. Among other things, Kevin did not feel free to reveal to his parents that he was gay. He had reason to fear that they could not accept what they would see as a flaw in the family image.

In combination with the above four limitations in many of our troubled families, there were for some of us three other circumstances that further limited our opportunities to meet basic human needs.

5. There was verbal abuse or physical violence at home. Verbal abuse or physical violence in our families added significantly to our fear as children. Violence magnified the impact of other destructive factors. The emotional and physical violence we encountered included hostile silences; deliberate failure to respond to others' requests; putdowns or sarcasm; name-calling and humiliation; intimidation; breaking things; dangerous driving; harsh spanking; pushing, shoving, slapping and hitting; and, at the extreme, using or threatening others with objects or weapons.

From Abuse To Passivity

Gail's father beat her mother, who slapped and hit Gail, particularly when she was a teenager. Her mother was threatened by Gail's attractiveness and found fault with all of Gail's achievements. When Gail rebelled, her mother became enraged, and Gail was terrified to resist her mother's assaults. She learned that she had to be passive about protecting herself, and as a result she was mistreated by her teenage friends and her first husband.

6. We lost parents through divorce or death. The loss of a parent through divorce or death greatly increased the probability that we would not receive the emotional and physical affection we needed because of the coping process of the remaining parent. Single parents frequently had a hard time financially, and this added greatly to family stress. Divorce exposed some of us to difficult choices of loyalty and closeness, and we often felt compelled to ally ourselves with one or the other parent.

A Feeling Of Abandonment

Emily's parents divorced when she was ten, after her alcoholic father abandoned the family. Emily had been very close to him, so it was an extreme blow to her to be left and seemingly forgotten. Her mother struggled very hard financially and never remarried. She resented Emily, who physically resembled her father and served as a reminder of that painful relationship. Even though she desperately needed affection, Emily grew up feeling that she could not trust anyone emotionally.

7. Our families had problems with sexual boundaries. Sexual boundaries, or appropriate limits on sexual information, talking or behavior, are always the responsibility of adults, not children. Children have sexual curiosity but are not motivated toward adult sexual behavior on their own (Miller, 1984). Sexual boundary problems include an absence of appropriate sexual education; inappropriate or humiliating communications to children about sexuality; and the following behaviors: parental sexual affairs, exposure to pornography, nudity and covert seduction, inappropriate touching and actual sexual activities. In extreme cases, sadistic or violent sexual activity is directed toward children. Sexual boundary problems in families have profound and enduring destructive impact in terms of identity, self-worth and future sexual behavior.

Confused Sexuality

Stan was traumatized as an early teenager when he learned that his mother was having an affair. He witnessed his father publicly confronting his mother and her lover, and he felt overwhelmed with feelings of humiliation. At that age, he was emotionally unprepared to understand this event. He was naive about sex and just beginning to notice girls. His mother's affair left him with a feeling of contempt for women and a later tendency to degrade women with whom he became sexual. His own natural developmental acceptance of sexuality had been shattered.

Image 2 portrays the dilemma we face as children growing up in troubled families (p. 19).

Additional Childhood Influences

Each of us was born with a unique set of personal characteristics. We also acquired certain sociocultural patterns in our families and communities. Our personal characteristics and sociocultural setting certainly affected the overall quality of our childhood environment.

The Reluctant Air Traffic Controller. *As children, many of us faced family situations that we were not prepared to handle. We had no choice but to do the best we could to cope with these situations. Here, a child tries to assume great responsibility without the support, training, understanding or maturity to perform in a very challenging situation. We may have done a competent job in our family even without resources, but because we lacked real readiness, our successes were often accompanied by anxiety and feelings of inadequacy.*

Our Personal Characteristics

As children, we responded to our parents and they responded to each of us in individual ways. From birth onward, our temperament and abilities were important in determining how we were treated in our family. Some of us were more demanding than others due to our energy level, strength of will, personality traits, sleeping patterns or overall physical health.

We assumed that we were being treated as unique individuals by the significant people in our lives. In troubled families, this was quite often simply not true. We may have reminded either or both parents of each other, their parents, or other persons with either positive or negative associations, and how they treated us may have been influenced by these associations. Frequently we learn later in life that something in a parent's past was important in determining his or her feelings about and treatment of us.

Understanding Her Father's Past

Cora always felt that her father went out of his way to be mean to her. When she was no longer a little girl, he no longer seemed to be warm and affectionate to her. Cora was confused, and she began to feel profoundly unworthy because he didn't love her. She tried very hard to please her father by her many accomplishments at school, but his rejection was unrelenting.

As an adult, when she began to research her family history, Cora learned that her father's mother had been mentally ill and had beaten him viciously before she was put into long-term care at the state hospital. Cora realized that her father had unconsciously punished her because of his unresolved rage from childhood. Cora could stop blaming herself for his rejection once she understood that her father's behavior was really that of the hurt and angry little boy within her father.

The Influence Of Culture

How we fared at any given time in our families was often significantly influenced by outside factors: the variety of people plus the social, educational, recreational and cultural resources in our communities. In addition, cultural patterns relating to work, relationships, independence, fun, alcohol and drugs, food and sex predisposed many of us to particular behavior patterns that began when we were children.

For example, "working hard" and "being kind" are two seemingly worthwhile practices that have led to painful results for some of us who grew up in troubled families. Emphasis on achievement benefits society, but this cultural pattern also contributes to compulsive working, resulting in great sacrifices in family relationships or health. Similarly, being kind and considerate and helping others are encouraged and respected in this culture, particularly for women. Excessive attempts to be kind, however, are frequently made at one's own expense, with potentially severe consequences. (Compulsive working and relationship dependency are discussed in Chapter 5.)

Evaluating Your Childhood Circumstances

What were the strengths and problem characteristics of your family when you were a child? You can rate your family using the following 2-10 scale (consider odd numbers as midpoints): 2 = very untrue of my family, 4 = moderately untrue of my family, 6 = slightly true of my family, 8 = moderately true of my family and 10 = very true of my family.

Family Strengths   **Rating**

1. My parents enjoyed their marriage and their children.   _2_

2. In my family, we talked with each other and were interested in what everyone had to say.   4,5 _3_

3. We respected and supported each other when we were hurt or having problems.   _2_

4. I knew that I could trust and rely on the people in my family.   _3_

5. Responsibility was shared reasonably and fairly between my parents and among the kids.   _2_

6. We enjoyed spending time with each other and regularly did things together as a family.   _2_

7. My family taught me clear-cut values about right

and wrong.   2

8. We had regular family activities and traditions.   2

Total   18

Family Problem Characteristics   **Rating**

1. My relationships with my parents and my siblings were emotionally unpredictable — sometimes close and sometimes distant.   10

2. As a child, I was given or felt I needed to take a great deal of adult responsibility before I was ready for it.   10

3. I did not receive the kind of tenderness and affection that I needed.   6

4. I was not watched over appropriately and was given either too much or too little freedom.   4

5. I didn't feel free to talk to other family members or to people outside my family about the problems I was having or the kinds of things that were going on at home.   10

6. There was verbal or physical violence toward me or others in my family while I was growing up.   10

7. My parents were divorced or I lost one of my parents through death when I was still at home.   10

8. Our family had problems with inappropriate sexual boundaries while I was growing up.   10

Total   70

Your Scores

The total possible score on each scale is 80. A score of 60 or more on *family strengths* indicates that you had significant resources available to you as a child. Scores between 40 and 60 suggest that your family had moderate strengths available to you to help offset family problem characteristics. Scores below 40 suggest that you were deprived of many of the family resources you needed.

A score of 32 or more on *family problem characteristics* indicates that you probably faced considerable trauma and deprivation during childhood. Healing from trauma and deprivation takes time; if this is true of you, you should allow yourself to move a little more slowly through recovery than a person who did not face this much traumatic stress. If you have a lower total family problem score, particular questions may highlight for you which destructive factors you faced. You may want to focus on these during your recovery work.

Chapter 3 discusses how limiting family environments caused us to develop only certain dimensions of ourselves. These limitations often continued so that we became partially functioning adults prone to compulsive behavior patterns. As we come to understand our behavior patterns and obtain *clarity* about how and why these came into being, we regain control of our choices and our lives.

3. SURVIVING IN TROUBLED FAMILIES

We find the roots of our repetitive adult patterns in our limiting childhood environments. As children, we were able to survive even extreme difficulties, but we usually paid a significant price. We had very little power, experience or information to work with, and we did not have the option of leaving our families (Greenleaf, 1981). Our need to survive prevailed.

We retain from childhood emotional and behavioral strategies that were ingenious solutions to the dilemmas we faced at the time. These same strategies may appear to improve our situation as adults, but in fact our old choices frequently make things worse. For example, we often learned as children that it was not in our best interests to feel the emotional impact of certain events. We learned to shut our emotions off in order to preserve the illusion that things were okay. As adults, however, we lose critical information that we need for decision making when we don't allow ourselves to feel.

One of our goals in recovery from compulsive patterns is to move from illusion-based to knowledge-based decision making. Part of our new knowledge base is the understanding that we had to make the best of our difficult childhood situations. This chapter describes our resourceful childhood strategies.

Our Childhood Survival Strategies

Table 3.1 (see p. 27) presents the aims, behavioral strategies, protective emotional strategies and self-comforting behavior we developed growing up in a troubled family system. The term *strategy* does not imply that we planned these ways of coping. Our behavior in our troubled family resulted both from being cast in certain roles by the family and from our attempts to make things better. For instance, oldest children are often selected by themselves and their parents to take responsibility and achieve. As older siblings leave home, younger children may take over these roles.

Our Childhood Aims

Our behavior as children in troubled families can usually be understood in terms of two natural yet unconscious aims:

1. We generally behaved in ways that served to meet our basic human needs if the opportunity was available.
2. We usually tried to avoid or improve painful or dangerous situations.

Common Behavioral Strategies

Common behavioral strategies in troubled families have been described by family therapists working with alcoholic family systems (Wegscheider, 1981; and Black, 1981). Five strategies that are most frequently pursued are:

1. Taking responsibility and focusing on achieving
2. Caretaking and controlling in relationships
3. Rebelling and creating problems
4. Adapting or becoming invisible
5. Remaining dependent or under-responsible

Your Behavioral Strategies

Most of us used several different strategies as our families changed or older siblings left home. In very troubled family

Table 3.1. Child Survival Strategies in Troubled Families

Child Aims	Protective Emotional Strategies	Behavioral Strategies	Self-Comforting Behaviors
Meeting basic human needs such as: Physical health Safety and security Love and affection Self-esteem Etc.	Utilizing defense mechanisms	Taking responsibility and achieving	Engaging in satiation behaviors such as: Eating Watching television
	Distorting reality self-protectively using the emotional discounting process	Caretaking and controlling in relationships	Engaging in arousal behaviors such as: Physical exertion Risk-taking Masturbation
		Rebelling or creating problems	
Avoiding or improving painful or dangerous situations		Adapting or becoming invisible	Engaging in fantasy behaviors such as: Reading Fantasy life in daydreaming
		Remaining dependent or under-responsible	

systems, however, we may have been locked into a particular pattern. You can use the following scale to evaluate which strategies you relied on most heavily as a child. Rate each statement using the 2-10 scale: 2 = very untrue of me, 4 = moderately untrue of me, 6 = slightly true of me, 8 = moderately true of me and 10 = very true of me.

Taking Responsibility and Focusing on Achieving   Rating

1. My responsibilities as a child went beyond what I was developmentally prepared for.   _4_

2. One of the main ways that I felt good about myself was by being acknowledged for being responsible.   _8_

3. I tried very hard and did well in school or in activities like sports, clubs or jobs.   _8_

4. I had the feeling that I was a failure as a person if I did not do really well at something.   _8_

   Total   _28_

Caretaking and Controlling in Relationships   Rating

1. I took or was given a lot of responsibility for other family members as a child.   _8_

2. I tried to counsel or help one or both of my parents with their problems.   _8_

3. I gave advice or orders to my parents or my siblings in an effort to get them to do what I thought would make things go better in the family.   _6_

4. I learned to be a good listener and found that others would come to me for help.   _6_

   Total   _28_

Rebelling or Creating Problems   Rating

1. I often got into trouble at home because I wouldn't go along with things that I didn't think were right.   _2_

2. I tended to express feelings in groups that other people also felt but didn't acknowledge.   _2_

3. I was angry as a child and did things that were destructive to myself or others as a result.   _3_

4. I got into trouble at school and in the community because I did things without caring what happened. _2_

Total _9_

Adapting and Becoming Invisible Rating
1. I spent a lot of time by myself as a child because
that was more comfortable than being around my
family. _10_
2. I found that the best thing to do was to keep quiet
and let things blow over, so I tried to become
invisible to others. _10_
3. I always wanted someone to seek me out and care
about me because I often felt lonely. _10_
4. I received acknowledgment for not being a bother;
this was one way of feeling good about myself even
though I wanted more. _8_

Total _38_

Remaining Dependent or Under-responsible Rating
1. I was not encouraged to grow up and be responsible. _2_
2. One or both of my parents regularly did things for
me that I needed to do for myself. _2_
3. I was not disciplined firmly and got away with
things that I shouldn't have as a child. _2_
4. I learned to manipulate other family members into
doing what I wanted them to do. _2_

Total _8_

Your Scores

Total your scores for each pattern. Pattern scores can range
from 8 to 40. A score of 24 or above indicates that you strongly
relied on a particular strategy as a child.

Our Protective Emotional Strategies

As children, we needed to protect ourselves emotionally to
maintain equilibrium as we faced the possibilities of abandon-

ment, injury or destroyed families. Our most basic defense as children against painful emotional or environmental developments was to deny them. *We chose to not see things as they were* (Ossorio, 1976). By this means, we could buy time (perhaps years) until we were more able to understand and integrate those events. Unfortunately, the longer we fail to understand and integrate our painful realities, the longer we suffer from them.

The denial process has been most clearly described by Jacqui Lee Schiff as *emotional discounting* (1975). She identified four levels of discounting that we use to spare ourselves from confronting potentially devastating emotional situations immediately:

1. We discount the *existence* of a problem.
2. We discount the *significance* of a problem, downplaying its *intensity* or *importance*.
3. We discount the *possibility of changing* a problem.
4. We discount our *own abilities* and blame ourselves.

Surviving Fear

Christina, a teenager, felt trapped in her family. Her parents fought bitterly and pulled her into their conflicts. Christina described their extremely violent scenes in an unemotional manner because she had regularly discounted the intensity and significance of these family crises. She felt helpless to change the situation, and although she wanted to leave home, she felt guilty about abandoning the people she loved. Christina criticized herself and concluded that she was a burden to her parents and part of the cause of their problems. As a first step in recovery, Christina learned to accept that her parents' problems were of their own making. She saw how she had discounted her own feelings and needs in order to survive. Christina gradually realized the extent of her fear and finally moved in with an aunt and uncle, with whom she could feel safe and secure.

Unfortunately, we tend to continue discounting after we leave our troubled family systems. Our adult discounting may contribute to our entrapment in unsatisfying patterns. As we overcome compulsive behavior patterns, we often must reexamine our past circumstances and see their true emotional significance. As we develop a new and honest emotional relationship with the past, we increase our ability to see present situations more clearly and act with greater emotional freedom.

Discounting Exercise

Identify the types of discounting that you use the most in dealing with problems in your life. A good way to do this is to keep a daily log for a few weeks. You will need a few minutes of privacy every day for self-observation.

Examine the events of the day and determine if you have discounted your feelings. Spend a little time, as well, thinking about events of childhood. Today or as a child did you: (1) discount the existence of a problem, (2) discount its intensity or significance, (3) discount the possibilities for change or (4) discount your own ability and blame yourself?

Begin to be conscious of situations in which you say, "No problem," "I didn't even notice," "That's okay," "No big deal," "I don't care," "There is nothing I can do about it," "I guess I deserved it," or "I can't do anything right." Notice subtle distress cues that you get inside when you discount your feelings. Maybe that *did* bother you. Maybe there *is* something you can do about it. Maybe it was *not* your fault. Stopping habitual discounting is part of the recognition process that prepares you to take positive action in your life.

Self-Comforting Behavior

We comforted ourselves as children using whatever was available to us. Actions we commonly chose fall into three behavior categories: *Satiation, arousal* and *fantasy* (Milkman and Sunderwirth, 1982). Examples of satiation behavior are eating, sleeping and watching television. Arousal behavior includes intense physical exertion, masturbation or physical risk-taking. Fantasy behavior includes reading comic books or pulp novels or daydreaming. At times, in difficult environments, we comforted ourselves to an extreme in these ways. Our childhood self-comforting style points us toward certain adult escapes that we may turn to later.

Your Self-Comforting

How did you comfort yourself as a child? Did you rely on certain self-comforting behaviors? Number the actions below from 1 to 9, with 1 indicating the most reliance on that action in relation to the others and 9 indicating the least reliance:

_2_	eating
_1_	sleeping
_5_	watching television
_7_	exerting self physically
_6_	masturbating
_8_	taking physical risks
_3_	reading
_4_	daydreaming
___	other? _____

Our childhood self-comforting strategies often provide the basis for the kinds of escapes that we choose later as adults. We will discuss this more in Chapter 6.

Lisa's Rebellion

Lisa, a 34-year-old businesswoman, described her difficulty with authority figures: "I respond to anyone who I think is trying to control me with rebellion. I have to deal with a lot of pushy people in my professional life. I feel like telling them off and walking out. I don't say what I am thinking that often, but I come close. I am angry a lot. I keep myself calm with alcohol.

"I want to maintain responsibility for myself, but I need help from someone. I am afraid I'm going to fail professionally because I undermine myself. I just got a promotion, and I have to cut back on my drinking."

Lisa's Childhood Oppression

Lisa had to deal with her mother's unreasonable use of authority when she was little. During childhood, her father worked away from home for months at a time. Lisa seldom did anything to provoke her, but her mother was bitter and angry most of the time. Her mother seemed to resent her, and Lisa felt consistently misunderstood and mistreated.

Lisa tried to escape her mother's coercive control by spending a lot of time alone and creating a fantasy world for herself. She preferred loneliness to being treated in a dictatorial manner. Lisa resented her mother's habit of taking credit for Lisa's school and sports successes, robbing Lisa of her own satisfaction and sense of self-worth. The only way she could find to express anger and assert her autonomy was to stop trying and fail at things that she knew her mother particularly wanted. This unconscious conflict left her feeling bad and ashamed.

Lisa anxiously awaited her father's return as the solution to her loneliness. When he did come back, however, he was always preoccupied with work, and Lisa did not have the closeness she hoped for.

In her professional life, Lisa found that she constantly fought her urge to rebel and create conflict where she worked. She found it harder and harder to complete the projects she was assigned because she resented her superiors taking credit for her work. Beginning as a young adult, Lisa began to suppress her painful conflicts by drinking.

Recovery Healing

During recovery, Lisa recognized how hurt she was and how angry she felt toward her mother. Through a women's group, she found that she could trust some people not to violate her right to self-determination. With therapy and self-help groups, she received some of the nurturing and support that she had craved from her father. She decided in the course of recovery to abstain completely from alcohol.

Lisa had developed great professional competence but had never developed real self-respect because she was constantly tempted to sabotage her success and covertly express anger. As Lisa recognized the source of her anger, she no longer needed to hold herself back from success.

Becoming Fully Functioning Adults

Our childhood foundations were severely lacking for many of us. In our efforts to have our basic human needs met, we utilized limited behavioral strategies. The result was that many of us arrived at adulthood out of balance — compelled to act in certain ways rather than free to be ourselves. *Compulsion* is characterized by continuing use of a single action or pattern of behavior until it detracts from our well-being. In contrast, *freedom* means that we are able to choose from our available choices and enhance our long-term best interests. With behavioral freedom, we can achieve a satisfactory balance between four value perspectives: *practical, ethical, pleasurable* and *tasteful* (Ossorio, 1977). As an example, let's look at friendship behavior from each of these perspectives.

We behave practically when we do something realistic and efficient such as being on time for an appointment with friends or returning a book we borrowed.

Ethical behavior means doing the right thing rather than cutting corners. In our friendships, we behave ethically when we let other people know honestly where they stand with us.

Pleasurable behavior is enjoyable for either immediate or symbolic reasons. In friendships, we enjoy sharing meals in pleasant surroundings, and we appreciate the lighthearted exchange about our experiences since we were last together. We feel good when other people communicate clearly that they are our friends.

Tasteful behavior is pleasing in terms of its sensitivity, excellence, beauty or eloquence. We are touched when friends remember us on our birthdays and when the gifts selected for us were carefully chosen to fit with our own interests and tastes.

Recovery means gaining the freedom and ability to include a good mix of practicality, ethics, pleasure and tastefulness in our lives. Compulsive patterns involve neglecting one or more of these dimensions of behavior.

If we work compulsively, we may overemphasize practical dimensions of behavior at the expense of pleasurable and tasteful possibilities. The birthday gift for a friend selected by one's secretary is practical but does not fulfill the requirements of pleasurable and tasteful behavior. If we struggle with perpetual-child syndrome, we may underemphasize the practical and overemphasize the pleasurable and tasteful dimensions. A surprise night out at an expensive restaurant, for example, becomes yet another irritant to a spouse who is already concerned about paying the bills.

Having matured in environments that required survival behavior and did not allow for balance, we usually have some growing to do as we broaden our values and learn new and necessary skills. To make these changes, we need new support systems and new teachers. "Family of choice" is a term coined by Sharon Wegscheider-Cruse to describe our ability as adults to find people who can support us and teach us the skills and values that we were unable to develop in our families of childhood. To create our families of choice, we must take responsibility for our own lives and needs and seek people who can give us what we need. We no longer have to try to make our families of childhood give us something they may not have. Emancipation from our families of childhood usually involves both loneliness and grief, but we can ultimately design relationships with our families that are respectful to both them and ourselves.

Image 3 portrays our struggles with our families of childhood. As young adults, we unsuccessfully attempt to wrest from them what we know families are supposed to provide (p. 36).

The Waterhole Gone Dry. *A desert scene portrays our sometimes desperate attempts to find the validation, support, protection and love that we have always wanted and needed in our families of childhood. A dried-up waterhole represents the unfortunate reality that we frequently encounter. There may once have been good water there, or perhaps there was just enough water to allow survival, but now the waterhole is dry. The discouragement resulting from this discovery can weaken us further. We must save our strength for the task we now face: to cross the desert to the oasis where the resources we need are available.*

4. PROBLEM EMOTIONAL ADJUSTMENTS

Many of us experienced a certain relief as we grew up and left our homes, glad that we made it out of our troubled family environments. Ironically, the defenses we used to survive and the emotional consequences of our childhood experiences continued to shape our adult choices. Physical separation from our families of childhood usually was not accompanied by emotional independence. We often unconsciously perpetuated the same environmental patterns that we wished to escape.

The first adult problems that concern us on our journey from compulsion to freedom are our problem emotional adjustments: *low self-esteem, unresolved emotions* and *difficulty trusting.* These adjustments limit our choices and underlie compulsive life patterns and compulsive escapes. As we recover, we must ultimately face these painful feelings. Using our new recovery resources, we can transform these old companions.

Low Self-Esteem

Low self-esteem is one of the most subtle and pervasive effects of our troubled families. It can show up in many forms during adulthood: lack of confidence, self-criticism, feelings of unworthiness, perfectionism, grandiosity, withdrawal, self-

sabotage and inability to take risks. Many of us fear trying
anything new because we anticipate humiliation. We find
ourselves frequently in a state of anxiety.

As we saw in Chapter 3, our families may have provided
many possible sources of low self-esteem. We may have been
treated unpredictably and inconsistently by our parents and
siblings; as a result, we failed to develop a sense of our own
worth and saw the world as a confusing place. We often took
on responsibilities for which we were unprepared, with a
resulting fear of failure and fear of exposure of our inadequa-
cies. If we were victims of verbal or physical violence, we
may later repeat to ourselves the explicit or implicit parental
messages that we received about our worth. It was usually
safer to blame ourselves than to conclude, "My father doesn't
love me," "My mother is crazy," or "Something is terribly
wrong with my family." Concluding that we were wrong
allowed us to try to improve ourselves, which gave us hope.

When we attempt to meet adult challenges and responsibilities
with impaired self-confidence and a critical internal dialogue, we
feel terribly afraid that we will be exposed as inadequate. *Shame*
is one of the most powerful dimensions of our low self-esteem.
Gershen Kaufman describes this painful emotion: "Contained in
the experience of shame is the piercing awareness of ourselves as
fundamentally deficient in some way as a human being. To live
with shame is to experience the very essence or heart of the self
as wanting" (1980). We arrange our lives to avoid such painful
exposure at any cost. We practice "image management," which
emphasizes looking good on the outside regardless of our true
emotional or family situation. In other words, we put up a good
front no matter what.

In a society that emphasizes and competes for the external
trappings of success, power, youth, wealth and happiness,
many of us experience a *shame gap*. This is the discrepancy
between the public image of status, power, confidence and
success that we may attempt to convey and the private truth
about our emotional lives, intimate relationships and compulsive behavior patterns.

Hurting On The Inside

Paula was a successful executive who secretly felt unworthy. She had been adopted as a child but never knew it

until she was told by a stranger when she was in high school. She was then humiliated by other students at school. This experience caused deep feelings of hurt, betrayal and shame. Paula vowed to herself that by her achievements she would demonstrate to her family and community that she was better than they. Her success was empty, however, because she could not acknowledge and heal from her deep pain. She had also developed a problem with alcohol. Her vulnerability and addiction were inconsistent with the image that she wished to convey to her childhood persecutors. Paula had to face her adolescent pain and learn to validate and care for herself.

There are powerful cultural prohibitions against the admission of failure, whether great or small. In order to recover, however, we have to overcome our image management and shame. We must be prepared to confront, *with compassion,* the truth about ourselves and our lives as we grow toward well-being. The ingredients of compassion are: (1) an understanding of the power of the forces that compelled us in troubled families, (2) the knowledge that other people struggle with the same dilemmas and (3) the hope that we can change our lives for the better.

Your Self-Esteem

Use the following scale to evaluate your self-esteem: 2 = very untrue of me, 4 = moderately untrue of me, 6 = slightly true of me, 8 = moderately true of me and 10 = very true of me.

Your Self-Esteem	Rating
1. I feel confident about my ability to do the things I must to improve my life.	2
2. I am able to give myself the benefit of the doubt if I make mistakes.	3
3. I feel basically worthy as a person.	2
4. I am able to take risks and try new things without having to do them well right away.	2
5. I feel good about the way I do my job.	8
6. The way I appear to others pretty well matches how I feel about myself inside.	6

7. I have compassion for myself and the way my life has developed. $\underline{2}$

8. I deserve the good things in my life. $\underline{8}$

   Total $\underline{33}$

Your Scores

Scores on this scale can range from 16 to 80. A score of 40 or below indicates that low self-esteem is a significant problem for you. If your score is between 40 and 60, you have moderate self-esteem. A score between 60 and 80 implies that you have high self-esteem. If you have low or moderate self-esteem, you might consider beginning to replace your critical internal messages with self-affirmations. You can use Rokelle Lerner's book, *Daily Affirmations for Adult Children of Alcoholics*, for this purpose on a daily basis. You may want to return to this self-esteem scale from time to time during your recovery to see the progress you have made.

Unresolved Emotions

Like Paula, we may carry with us unresolved feelings of hurt, disappointment, shame, guilt, loss, anger or grief from our troubled families. We often did not have the safety and opportunity as children to process the true emotional significance of events in our lives.

Feeling unloved or unwanted or experiencing constant conflict, the death or loss of a parent or sibling, family violence or sexual boundary problems all had great emotional significance, but we habitually discounted the emotional impact of these childhood traumas in order to protect ourselves. As adults, we continue to discount the emotional significance of similar situations. This defensive evaluation of reality can lead to emotional numbness or shallowness; we don't allow ourselves to feel anything, or we keep our feelings from going too deep. Alternatively, we may become hyper-sensitive to rejection, conflict, anger, inconsistency or sexuality. We may fear emotions and feel poorly prepared for life, which naturally involves losses, transitions, trauma and conflict. We may see normal setbacks as insurmountable and decide that our situation is hopeless.

Our first task as young adults was to move into an independent sphere in the larger world — sometimes a frightening
experience. To put off leaving, some of us made rather
desperate attempts to change our families for the better. We
found it difficult to accept that we could not make them
change. When we did leave home, we may have had to learn
the difference between rebelling against and being independent of our families. Some of us spend the rest of our lives
trying desperately *not* to be like our parents in any way. We
may discard the strengths that we developed in an effort to
correct the deficits we experienced. Such rebellion indicates
unfinished separation. To achieve true separation, we must be
able to freely choose ways of life that suit us individually.

Your Unresolved Emotions

The following scale will help you evaluate the role of
unresolved emotions in your life. Use the 2-10 scale: 2 = very
untrue of me, 4 = moderately untrue of me, 6 = slightly true of
me, 8 = moderately true of me and 10 = very true of me.

Your Unresolved Emotions	**Rating**
1. Many things happened during my childhood that I just didn't let myself feel.	8
2. I find myself overreacting to situations that touch old feelings.	8
3. I often think that I am better off not expecting too much so that I won't be disappointed if things don't work out.	8
4. I often become depressed without really under-standing why.	10
5. I often don't know what I really feel and need.	10
6. I'm still trying to help or change my parents or fam-ily so that they will be more like the family I need.	8
7. I am afraid to let myself feel too deeply because I fear that I might fall apart.	6
8. I have been trying to be completely different from the way one or both of my parents are or were.	8
Total	66

Your Scores

Your score on this scale can range from 16 to 80. Any single item scored at 8 or above suggests an issue for you to explore during recovery. An overall score below 32 suggests that you are not significantly troubled by unresolved childhood emotions. A score of 32-56 implies that unresolved emotions may be interfering with your life to a moderate degree. A score of 56 or above suggests a possible need for a professional consultation about your unresolved emotions.

Difficulty Trusting

Alone or in combination, low self-esteem and unresolved emotions have great impact on our relationships with ourselves, others and the world at large. Many of us grow up not believing that we could create meaningful lives, form lasting and satisfying relationships, and find a fulfilling place for ourselves in the world. We often enter our relationships with a great fear of abandonment. We are preoccupied with image management and shame about our histories and inner lives and thus create invisible distance from others, who usually respond by withdrawing. Thus we end up alone, telling ourselves that we knew all along that this would happen.

Acting from low self-esteem, we may choose people who do not treat us well. We are often poorly equipped to resolve conflicts in relationships because we fear anger, lack awareness of our needs and have difficulty expressing feelings. Unfinished separation from our childhood families drains the energy we have for adult relationships. The combined result of these emotional adjustments is that we often live in a state of fear. Our basic fear is that the world does not have a place for us (Ossorio, 1976). Patrick Carnes describes three core beliefs that underlie all compulsive behaviors (1983):

1. I am basically a bad, unworthy person.
2. No one would love me as I am.
3. My needs are never going to be met if I have to depend on others.

With such desperate feelings inside, we enter adulthood determined to escape our childhood dragons. Most of us absorb a great deal of painful life experience before we learn that we must ultimately confront these feelings we fear. We don't have to face our dragons alone, however. With the strength of our recovery resources, we never have to be alone and hopeless with our pain again.

Image 4 portrays our problem emotional adjustments from childhood (p. 44).

Ryan's Emancipation

Ryan had been divorced for six years and sought therapy when he met a woman he wanted to marry. "I want to understand myself and what went wrong in my marriage before I get into another bad relationship. I don't trust myself to make good decisions. I feel bad about the way I am running my life. My self-confidence is really poor.

"I grew up in a very strict family where I couldn't have my own ideas. My parents didn't seem to approve of anything I did. I rebelled inside but went along with what they wanted for me because inside I was lost. They wanted me to become a lawyer, but I wanted to be a creative writer. I ended up as a technical writer but I don't feel really respected for my work at my company."

Ryan's Problem Emotional Adjustments

Ryan's childhood environment of rejection and criticism was debilitating. He needed support, guidance and trust as he attempted to become independent and find his appropriate place in the world, but he felt that he had to adapt and become invisible to survive in his family. He learned to comfort himself by retreating into books and daydreams. His interest in becoming a writer grew out of these childhood activities. As an adult, he used marijuana to retreat into fantasy when his life became too painful.

As a young adult, Ryan did not know himself well and had not gained confidence through the process of his own trial-and-error decision making. With his first marriage, he attempted to create a substitute family, but his choice of a partner reflected his low self-esteem. He married a woman who became critical and unaccepting of him, and the relationship failed.

Our Inner Children Must Be Healed. *An old-fashioned camera reveals the inner children hidden behind our external signs of affluence and success. We must reconcile ourselves with these little boys and girls who carry the memories of childhood losses, hurts and disappointments. As our inner children are allowed to heal, the tremendous resources of our childhood selves become available to us. We can rediscover the spontaneity, humor, creativity, tenderness and love that are the natural experiences of childhood.*

Ryan's Healing Process

Ryan yearned to trust his own feelings about what was right for him, but he needed support. He found it through psychotherapy and self-help groups, where he could explore his anger and sadness about the things his parents couldn't give.

As he recovered, Ryan learned to be compassionate with himself about the process of his life. "I understand that I did pretty well in light of the fact that my parents couldn't accept me. I am ready to go on now and have the life I want to have." As a starting place, he decided to discontinue all drug use. Later, he began to consciously choose friends with whom he could be his best self. He saw that he needed a lot of recognition and appreciation from his family of choice.

Ryan understood that he had entered his profession expecting to be misunderstood and mistreated in the same way he was at home. He inadvertently set himself up for this by presenting himself at work in a self-deprecating way. As he felt better about himself, he was able to make a more positive self-presentation at work and was treated more respectfully as a result. He decided to pursue his new love relationship with his eyes open, without the illusion that she would be able to offset the hurts of the past. As his new life took shape, Ryan finally began to feel at peace with his parents. He was going on with his life and no longer needed to resent their failings.

5. COMPULSIVE LIFE PATTERNS

"**I** won't make the mistakes my parents made!" Many of us say this to ourselves as we launch into adulthood. With the natural optimism of youth, we apply our energy and strength to the achievements of "success" and "happiness." Unfortunately, our achievement may actually be compulsive life patterns that can sabotage our adult well-being. These patterns develop when we continue our childhood survival strategies during adulthood until we feel powerless to change them, even when they negatively affect our relationships and physical and emotional health.

How Compulsive Life Patterns Begin

Compulsive life patterns derive directly from our childhood survival behavioral strategies:

1. Taking responsibility and focusing on achieving can lead to *compulsive working*.
2. Caretaking and controlling in relationships can lead to *relationship dependency*.
3. Rebelling and creating problems can lead to *generalized rebellion*.
4. Adapting and becoming invisible can lead to *victim syndrome*.

5. Remaining dependent or irresponsible can lead to *perpetual-child syndrome*.

Robin Norwood has described relationship dependency for women in depth in her book *Women Who Love Too Much*, and Dan Kiley has identified perpetual-child syndrome for men in *The Peter Pan Syndrome*.

All forms of survival behavior involve skills that can be useful in families and society. For instance, rebelling and dealing with conflict form the foundation of the democratic process, and adapting and becoming invisible are important for efficient functioning in large and anonymous social units.

How, then, do these activities become compulsive? Claudia Black points out that for each child survival strategy, we learn certain skills but simultaneously neglect others (1981). For example, if we learn to take responsibility and achieve, we may not learn to ask for help and to trust. If we learn to be dependent or under-responsible, we may not learn how to take care of ourselves or follow through with commitments.

We become compulsive by overpracticing the skills we do have and neglecting the skills we have not practiced and mastered. The wider the "skill gap" becomes, the more we may fear that we can never learn the neglected skills.

There is an ironic trait of human nature at work here. When our strategy doesn't seem to work anymore, our first reaction is to do it more frequently and with more intensity. For example, when we encounter someone who is not treating us fairly, we may become angry. This does not seem to change their behavior toward us, so that we become even angrier and more demanding, perhaps shouting and making threats. On the other hand, we may respond to mistreatment by being increasingly accommodating, failing to notice that we are dealing with someone who is not acting in good faith. Recovery involves understanding such misguided strategies and substituting new behavior options.

By early adulthood, our behavioral skills and deficits are established, and certain choices become habitual. As our choices become habits, our habits become our reality, and through our reality we define ourselves and the world. In this way, we become deeply invested in remaining the same, even if that means remaining in pain and conflict. Unfortunately, many of us conclude that pain and conflict are normal and unavoidable.

As adults, we commonly make statements about ourselves, such as "I am a good student," "I am not very good at expressing my needs," "I don't understand men (women)," "I hate being told what to do," "I am very shy in new situations," or "Why should I do it if I can get someone to do it for me?" We seldom wonder how these aspects of our identity came into being; we just assume that we're stuck being that way.

Three factors are important in understanding how we continue certain child behavior strategies into adulthood until they become compulsive life patterns:

1. We commonly have a mistaken belief (relating to childhood circumstances) that this behavior will lead to achieving our goals.
2. Each behavior pattern results in certain intermittent rewards that reinforce the pattern.
3. Continuing our survival behavior allows us to avoid painful feelings and problems.

As our compulsive life patterns progress, we overinvest in survival behavior patterns and underinvest in behavior that would allow us to meet other basic human needs. Over time, we become painfully aware of certain psychological, physical and interpersonal complications that are the results of our behavior patterns, but because we feel the need to survive, there does not appear to be any chance for change. The irony of this is that by perpetuating our childhood survival behavior patterns, we create unbalanced situations in adult life that indeed need to be survived.

Many of us have a particular life pattern that is most troublesome for us, but we usually have some characteristics from other patterns as well. For instance, we may work compulsively in our professional life but at the same time behave according to perpetual-child syndrome in an intimate relationship. Major compulsive life patterns are described in the following section.

Five Compulsive Life Patterns

Clarity during recovery involves becoming conscious about our specific problem behaviors and complications so that we can begin to address these one by one as we grow. We can understand compulsive life patterns by identifying four central characteristics of each:

1. The *primary behavior* defines the pattern.
2. The *central obsession* preoccupies us with this pattern.
3. The *mistaken belief* perpetuates the pattern.
4. The *missing skills* make the pattern difficult to change.

Following the description of each pattern, a self-assessment allows you to rate characteristics from that pattern that are problems for you in your life.

Compulsive Working

1. **Primary behavior** is working more than 50 hours per week, considering one's occupation one's primary identity, working when one needs to spend time with family or friends, or neglecting health or rest because of work.
2. **Central obsession** is thinking about, planning for or worrying about work when not actively working.
3. **Mistaken belief** is saying, "If I just stay busy and continue to achieve I will be happy."
4. **Missing skills** are the ability to relax during unstructured time and the capacity to be emotionally close.

Underinvesting In His Marriage

"I know that my marriage is in trouble. My wife says this is because I spend too many hours at work. I just don't feel close to her anymore. She doesn't seem to understand what I have to do to make a living, and she is angry all the time."

As a self-employed salesperson, Todd was constantly aware that the more he worked, the more money he could make. As a child, he had not been a good student and because of this had often felt humiliated in school and in his family. He found his ability in sales to be a tremendous boost to his self-esteem, and he devoted more and more time to succeeding in his occupation. He began to spend his evenings and weekends making phone calls to line up appointments.

The result of Todd's overinvestment in work was an underinvestment in his marriage and family relationships, in caring for his health and in recreation. His business success was becoming meaningless because the other aspects of his life had been neglected. He suffered from migraine headaches and stomach problems. As time went on, Todd found himself less and less able to withdraw mentally from thinking or planning for work. He increased his cigarette smoking and relied on alcohol to unwind and fall asleep at night.

Todd's mistaken belief was, "If I am successful in sales I will be happy!" The intermittent rewards that he received from his work were self-esteem and recognition in the form of status and financial success. Todd's childhood motivation was an unconscious statement to those who had humiliated him: "I'll show you that I am somebody!" Constant activity allowed him to avoid feelings of emptiness and loneliness and provided distraction from the increasing consequences of his compulsive working. The more desperate these consequences became, the more compelled Todd felt to offset them with even greater professional achievements.

Image 5 portrays the childhood decision of a compulsive worker who denies himself other necessary aspects of life because of relentless striving (p. 52).

Compulsive Working Self-Assessment

If you feel that compulsive working is a pattern in your life, rate how the characteristics of the pattern apply to you. Use a 2-10 scale for each characteristic, where 2 = very untrue of me, 4 = moderately untrue of me, 6 = slightly true of me, 8 = moderately true of me and 10 = very true of me.

Your Compulsive Working Behavior   **Rating**

1. I work more than 50 hours per week. _4_
2. I consider my occupation my primary identity. _8_
3. I work even when I know that I need to spend time with my family or friends. _8_
4. I neglect my health or rest because of work. _2_
5. I think about, plan for or worry about work even when I am not actively working. _6_

The Workaholic. *It is Sunday, July 4, and the compulsive worker is preparing diligently for the coming week. He feels some sense of loss at having to pass up the holiday fun, but he considers the demands of work too pressing to allow time for any frivolous activity. He is making yet another payment toward the long-term price of compulsive working — isolation, fatigue and deprivation.*

6. I equate happiness with my level of achievement.   _6_
7. I have difficulty relaxing during unstructured time.   _6_
8. I have difficulty being emotionally close.   _8_
   Total   _48_

Your Scores

The highest possible score on this self-assessment is 80. Single-item high scores or an overall score above 40 suggest you may have a problem with this pattern.

Relationship Dependency

1. **Primary behavior** is investing time, energy and affection in a relationship with a person who does not reciprocate equally; subordinating one's own wishes, needs and values in order to accommodate a partner; taking most or all of the responsibility for the problems in a relationship; or worrying more about the other person's problems than he or she worries about him or herself.
2. **Central obsession** is thinking, worrying or planning how to improve a relationship.
3. **Mistaken belief** is saying, "If I care for someone enough, they will start to care about me."
4. **Missing skills** are awareness of personal feelings and needs and ability to protect oneself from criticism or abuse.

Fear Of Rejection

"I couldn't get my husband to come in with me. I know that we need marital counseling, but he does not believe in therapy or psychology. I finally decided to just come for myself."

Rebecca was depressed, anxious and angry. She was often sick with colds and flu and required back surgery due to low-back problems. Married for 20 years, she had felt for some years that her love was not reciprocated. The relationship was characterized by her husband's frequent criticism, and she had received little affection or sexual attention. Her long-term strategy had been to extend herself more and more for her husband, making an extreme effort to be attentive and considerate of his needs. She sought to set an example that would inspire him to be the husband she wanted him to be.

From time to time, Rebecca became extremely frustrated and lashed out at her husband. In response to these explosions, he would become more attentive for a time but afterward seemed to pull away even more. Abandonment was very frightening to Rebecca, and in response to his distance, she would soon begin "caretaking" again.

As time went on, Rebecca spent more time and energy preoccupied with and worried about her marriage. She continually encouraged her husband to read self-help books or seek counseling for himself, but he would not follow through. She gradually withdrew from her other friendships and community activities. She felt ashamed that she did not have the loving relationship that had always been a life goal for her. She did not sleep well and comforted herself by eating more until she became significantly overweight.

Rebecca's mistaken belief was, "I can love him enough to make him love and care for me." Her husband had grown up in an unaffectionate household. He was not motivated, or perhaps not able, to become a warm and giving person. In the early phases of the relationship, he was very responsive to her, and off and on he was sensitive and interested. Rebecca lived for these intermittent rewards, but she was emotionally starving in the marriage.

The childhood motivation behind her behavior had to do with rejection by her father and her determination to make her husband "love me and see how special I am." Rebecca's loneliness, anger and fear were terrifying to her because they were reminders of powerful childhood feelings of hopelessness. These feelings caused her to try desperately to make her marriage work in order to avoid facing painful reality.

Image 6 presents the common discrepancy between the romantic visions that couples unknowingly carry into a love relationship (p. 55).

Relationship Dependency Self-Assessment

Relationship dependency may be a problem for you. Rate to what extent the characteristics below apply to you using the same 2-10 scale you used for the compulsive working self-assessment.

His Dream/Her Dream. *The romantic couple is lost in the euphoria of "being in love." Each partner envisions someone who will fulfill his or her needs for attention and caring. His vision is of a woman who will cater to his every wish. Her vision is of romance and an elegant life together. Both envision themselves receiving. Eventually, the discrepancy between their visions becomes apparent.*

Your Relationship Dependency Behavior   **Rating**

1. I invest time, energy and affection in relationships
   in which these qualities are not reciprocated
   equally.   _10_

2. I subordinate my own wishes, needs and values in
   order to accommodate a partner.   _10_

3. I take excessive responsibility for the problems in a
   relationship.   _10_

4. I worry more about another person's problems than
   he or she does.   _8_

5. I spend much of my time thinking, planning or
   worrying about how to improve the relationship.   _8_

6. I believe that I can directly change another adult's
   feelings and behavior toward me.   _2_

7. I have trouble identifying my feelings and needs.   _8_

8. I feel unable to protect myself from criticism or
   abuse.   _6_

   Total   _62_

Your Scores

The total possible score on this scale is 80. High single-item
scores or an overall score above 40 suggests that you may have
a problem with this pattern.

Generalized Rebellion

1. **Primary behavior** is engaging in uninvited attempts to
   influence people and organizations; frequently taking a
   scapegoat or "fall guy" role in group situations; taking
   responsibility for things that are not appropriately one's
   concern; or using gentler persuasion at first, then turning
   to more aggressive tactics when others do not respond.
2. **Central obsession** is having anger over the irresponsibility or misbehavior of people or organizations.
3. **Mistaken belief** is saying, "My good intentions and
   efforts can overcome any problem."
4. **Missing skills** include ability to let issues pass without
   challenge if they do not directly involve oneself and ability
   to disengage from people or situations when it becomes
   apparent that one cannot directly influence them.

A Frustrating Campaign

"I am so angry about work that I can't sleep. I took a job in this government accounting office a year ago, just after I completed my CPA training. I was really excited about my career. I can't stand the political infighting and bureaucracy there. They are wasting a lot of the taxpayers' money. It drives me crazy!"

Joseph began a fruitless struggle to institute changes at work even though some of his concerns were not in his area of responsibility. His initial suggestions were received positively, but as time went on he encountered more resistance and gained a reputation as a troublemaker.

As a result of his campaigns over various issues, Joseph did not carry out his own duties completely, and his relationships with other staff members became quite strained. He took his work frustration home with him and as a result had more conflicts with his wife. He was not enjoying his life, and he spent a great deal of time smoking marijuana and watching TV in his free time.

Joseph's mistaken belief was, "I know how things could be better here and I can bring these changes about if I try hard enough." His intermittent success at instituting changes in the agency was rewarding enough to give him a sense of autonomy and self-esteem.

The roots of Joseph's present struggle were in his childhood attempts to improve the environment in his family. For years, he attempted to counsel his parents and tried without success to stop their violent arguments. His unconscious childhood resolve was, "I will make my family change, no matter what I have to do!" As Joseph confronted his failure to change his agency, he began to be aware of long-standing frustration and rage about his inability to help his family.

Image 7 portrays our long-term failure at changing painful realities that are not under our control (p. 58).

Generalized Rebellion Self-Assessment

Have you struggled with some lost causes and situations in which you felt powerless? If so, use the 2-10 scale to rate the extent to which the following characteristics apply to you.

The Lost Cause Graveyard. *A graveyard is the only appropriate resting place for many of the issues we fight in generalized rebellion. As adults, we unwittingly choose people and situations that we are powerless to change, thus duplicating the limitations of our childhood environment. The truth is that our ability to make people and organizations do what we want and need is very limited.*

Your Generalized Rebellion Behavior	Rating
1. I engage in uninvited attempts to influence people and organizations.	2
2. I frequently take the scapegoat or "fall guy" role in group situations.	2
3. I take responsibility for things that are not appropriately my concern.	2
4. I use gentler persuasion at first, then turn to more aggressive tactics when others do not respond.	2
5. I find myself preoccupied with the irresponsibility or misbehavior of people or organizations.	4
6. I believe that I can overcome any problem with good intentions and effort.	2
7. I have difficulty letting issues pass without challenge even if they do not directly involve me.	2
8. I find it hard to disengage emotionally even when it becomes apparent that I cannot directly influence others.	6
Total	22

Your Scores

The total possible score is 80. Single high scores or an overall score of 40 or above implies that you have a problem with this pattern.

Victim Syndrome

1. **Primary behavior** is participating naively or passively in situations that affect one's well-being; trying to get other people to take care of oneself; expressing hostility passively or indirectly in relationships; or letting authority figures such as parents, professionals or church authorities tell one what is best to do.
2. **Cental obsession** is preoccupation with the ways that one has been wronged.
3. **Mistaken belief** is saying, "If I just do what is right, other people will also."
4. **Missing skills** include awareness of personal feelings and needs and ability to directly assert one's own wishes and rights.

Just Doing Her Job

"I feel defeated. It seems like I can't cope with life. I was divorced four years ago after my husband abandoned us. He was violent with me and with my oldest son, and when I decided to go to the safehouse, he left us. Since that time I have had a hard time getting back on track."

Lynn was pale and showed little emotion as she described her life. Her four children lived with her, and she worked at a clerical job that didn't allow her to fully use her capabilities and education. Since the divorce, she had endured constant financial stress and had increased her hardship with some bad decisions on practical matters.

During her marriage, Lynn had devoted all of her energies to being a wife, mother and homemaker. Her ex-husband had never fully accepted career and financial responsibilities and increasingly had turned to alcohol as an escape. Lynn couldn't let herself see that her husband was not going to be the provider she had hoped for. She hoped that he would notice her obvious unhappiness and disappointment and start to change himself. But until she finally drew the line, their lives were characterized by conflict, violence and frequent crisis.

Having to take complete responsibility for herself and the children had always been a fearful prospect for Lynn. Her father had been a compulsive gambler, and she had lived on a roller coaster of financial ups and downs as a child. Lynn's childhood hope was, "If I just go along quietly and do my part, things will turn out all right."

Lynn had married young and invested herself totally in creating a nice home for her children. She had avoided developing her career and had never learned about some of the pitfalls of the adult world. Her mistaken belief was, "If I just do my job as a homemaker, he will provide for the family." During the early years of the marriage, she had maintained hope and achieved satisfaction and self-esteem by caring for her children and creating a warm home. Her child-rearing activities at home had provided distraction from the disruptions caused by her husband's irresponsibility and drinking.

Victim Syndrome Self-Assessment

If you feel victimized in a relationship or job situation, rate which characteristics of victim syndrome you experience in that situation. Use the 2-10 scale.

Your Victim Syndrome Behavior	Rating
1. I participate passively in situations that directly affect my well-being.	6
2. I hope I can find someone who will take care of me.	10
3. I let people know indirectly if I am unhappy about something.	6
4. I let authority figures in my life, such as parents, professionals or church authorities, tell me what is best for me.	10
5. I spend a lot of time thinking about how I have been wronged.	10
6. I believe that if I do what is right, other people will also.	4
7. I lack awareness of my own feelings and needs.	10
8. I do not know how to directly assert my own rights and wishes.	10
Total	66

Your Scores

The highest possible score is 80. Single high scores or an overall score of 40 implies that you may have a problem with this pattern.

Perpetual-Child Syndrome

1. **Primary behavior** is not following through on one's commitments; getting others to take care of one's own responsibilities; frequently asking that allowances be made for oneself, one's special circumstances or limitations; or finding that others are often angry because of one's behavior.
2. **Central obsession** is trying to find an easier way.
3. **Mistaken belief** is saying, "If I can get away with it or get someone else to do it for me I might as well," or "One should not have to work too hard at life."

4. **Missing skill** is taking responsibility for oneself.

Charming His Way Through Life

"My wife and I are separated because she discovered I was having an affair. This had been going on for about a year. I knew that I had to stop seeing the other person but hadn't been able to break things off. Things are not going well in my business, either. I started it about three years ago and it grew much faster than I anticipated. I overspent and got behind with the IRS. Now I can't seem to get out of debt."

Derek was an attractive and obviously talented person to whom people were naturally drawn. Many people had been willing to give him the benefit of the doubt in the past, but now their trust was wearing thin. It was a pattern for Derek to allow things to deteriorate before making a valiant effort to solve his problems. His new starts usually lasted for a short period of time before he began to neglect his responsibility and undermine his progress.

Derek's mistaken belief was, "If I really try hard for a while, then I can relax." As the youngest child in his family, his mother had been very close to Derek and had protected him from many of the consequences of his irresponsibility. He had learned that charm would get him through. The intermittent rewards of being a perpetual child came from the fact that other people tolerated his failure to follow through on his commitments, at least for a time.

The childhood decision behind Derek's behavior had to do with his relationship with his father, who never pushed Derek to achieve and gave him little support or acknowledgment. Derek's childhood conclusion became, "I do not have to really push myself and can just get by."

By the time Derek went through his cycle a number of times, he began to feel quite desperate and depressed. He turned to sexual affairs in order to relieve his distress, and as a result sowed the seeds for the next crisis.

Perpetual-Child Syndrome Self-Assessment

To what extent do you have characteristics of perpetual-child syndrome? If you have experienced some of these problems, rate which characteristics apply to you, using the 2-10 scale.

Your Perpetual-Child Behavior	Rating
1. I do not follow through on commitments.	4
2. I get others to take care of things that are really my responsibility.	2
3. I often ask that allowances be made for me or my special circumstances or limitations.	2
4. I often find myself in trouble with others because of my behavior.	2
5. I spend a lot of time thinking about how to avoid the drudgery of life.	4
6. I believe that if I can get away with something or get someone else to do it, I might as well.	2
7. I believe that I should not have to work too hard in life.	2
8. I have trouble taking responsibility for myself.	2
Total	20

Your Scores

The highest possible score on this scale is 80. Single high scores or an overall score of 40 or above implies that you may have a problem with this pattern.

Complications Of Compulsive Life Patterns

The five people described in this chapter were actively struggling with their compulsive life patterns. Their behavior patterns were no longer in their best interests, and their lives illustrate the complications that can develop from compulsive patterns:

1. Neglect of self-care, diet and exercise
2. Physical health problems such as illness, pain or muscle tension
3. Mental health problems such as depression, anxiety or insomnia
4. Family or marital conflict
5. Conflict with co-workers
6. Burnout symptoms such as cynicism, apathy or fatigue

7. Painful feelings such as shame, guilt, anger or disappointment

You will have an opportunity in Chapter 6 to evaluate the
severity of these complications in your life.

Reviewing Your Self-Assessments

Understanding your compulsive patterns is critical for your
recovery. During the next five days, try to examine a different
compulsive life pattern each day and ponder how it may
relate to you. You might take 15 minutes after dinner each
evening to read the characteristics of one life pattern and then
examine that day and the recent past for examples from your
life that fit those characteristics. In this way you can attain
clarity about your particular blend of compulsive life patterns.
This understanding will greatly aid you in moving from
compulsion toward freedom.

6. COMPULSIVE ESCAPES

As human beings, we naturally seek changes in consciousness. To achieve a satisfying and lasting state of mind and body is a basic life challenge. Our states of mind and awareness can differ subtly or dramatically, changing quickly or over long periods. We achieve subtle changes in consciousness by actions such as taking a hot shower in the morning, eating a tasteful and satisfying meal, completing a project at work, watching a beautiful sunset, working out at a health club or playing with children in the evening. Distinct changes in consciousness result from actions such as using alcohol or drugs, smoking cigarettes, over- and undereating, having sex, running a marathon, attending a moving church service, buying clothes, taking risks in dangerous sports or gambling.

The more distress we feel, the more we rely on distinct and immediate changes in consciousness. These escapes can become compulsive when we choose them over and over until we feel unable to stop, even when we harm ourselves. By compulsively escaping, we create significant new emotional, health and relationship problems.

Why We Seek Escapes

Emotional, biological, family and cultural factors all contribute to the development of escape patterns. For most of us, pain resulting from our problem emotional adjustments and compulsive life patterns contributes to our relief-seeking behavior. Our families, communities and society all teach us about escapes: (1) our parents modeled "appropriate" escapes for us when we were children, (2) as teenagers we shared our discoveries about escapes, and (3) our society bombards us with possible avenues of escape.

Each of us has a unique body chemistry and differs from others in temperament and moods. Our individual well-being from conception onward reflects the influence of a multitude of factors as psychology and biology interact. Three psycho-biological factors normally contribute to the start of escape behavior:

1) We experience a state of mind or body (frequently negative) that we decide (consciously or uncon-sciously) to change.
2) We discover a behavior that "improves" that state of mind or body.
3) The personal consequences of this escape behavior are not immediately prohibitive for us.

Drinking To Escape

Greg was referred to therapy by his physician because his drinking was aggravating an ulcer. He was unhappy and worried after finding out that the job he had held for several years was being phased out by his company. Greg had always had a hard time dealing with change, and he said that he had been depressed most of his life.

Greg described his father as a beer drinker who was depressed and passive. He did not spend the time with Greg that his son needed as a little boy. Greg's mother was often angry because of her husband's passivity and was dissatisfied about the family's finances. Greg's grandfathers on both sides were alcoholics. In reaction to her childhood experiences, his mother did not drink at all.

Greg was awkward with and intimidated by girls as a teenager and found that when he drank he was much more confident. His humor and antics at parties gained him some acceptance with friends, and alcohol became a regular part of his social life. By his early 20s, Greg began to overdrink on occasion and sometimes passed out. After he was arrested for drunk driving, he tried to drink moderately but would periodically overdo it. His physician finally told him that he would have to stop drinking altogether because the alcohol was aggravating his stomach.

Finding A Favorite Escape

Our favorite escapes create feelings that we particularly value. When we discover an activity that may become a compulsive escape, we "fall in love" with it, so dramatic and positive is its impact on us (Cruse, 1984). Our favored escapes create biological interactions that we experience as "just right." With our escapes, we can suppress feelings of loneliness, inadequacy or shame and instead feel exactly the way we want. We describe our experiences in enthusiastic terms, such as, "When I drink I feel confident and powerful," "After having sex I feel good about myself," "When I parachute I feel really alive," or "While eating ice cream I feel peaceful and content."

Our adult escapes relate to our childhood self-comforting strategies. Using alcohol, taking tranquilizers, overeating and buying clothes are *satiation escapes*. Cocaine, amphetamines, physical risk-taking, gambling, cigarettes and sexual seduction are *arousal escapes*. Marijuana, movies, romantic or adventure novels and masturbation are *fantasy escapes*. We comfort ourselves in various ways as children, frequently choosing a favorite escape. During recovery, we replace our compulsive escapes one by one, stopping those that cause the most damage first.

A Cycle Of Eating, Vomiting and Fantasy

Dorothy's father was in the Army, and the family moved a number of times while she was in grade school. She hated to leave her friends and then try to fit into a new school. She was shy and fearful and often felt lonely, so that she created a fantasy world where she was surrounded by people who loved her.

Her parents fought bitterly with each other when Dorothy was little. She learned later that her father had had many sexual affairs. Dorothy felt her father was distant and critical with her. Her mother was overweight, and when Dorothy felt insecure or discouraged, her mother offered her something to eat. Dorothy associated eating with security in the midst of painful events. She developed a habit of taking snacks from the refrigerator and retreating to her room.

As a teenager, Dorothy ate to comfort herself even though her weight was embarrassing to her. She spent her free time reading romantic novels and dreaming of a relationship with a lover who would make her the envy of everyone.

Because she felt so ashamed of her weight, Dorothy began to induce vomiting as a way of making up for her binges. By adulthood, she was caught in a secret cycle of distress, eating, fantasy, guilt, vomiting and depression. Recovery for Dorothy began when she sought help to stop from having binges and vomiting. With support, she could face her underlying lone-liness and pain.

Through escape behavior we often communicate symbolic messages to others such as, "I guess I showed him or her!" or "Mom and Dad, if only you could see me now!" or "This is what you get for trying to control me!"

Investing In The Fast Lane

During high school, Anthony felt shut out socially by an in-group of wealthy kids. He resolved to "be somebody" so that no one could ever put him down again. He became a stockbroker after college and was intent on developing a six-figure income within five years. The excitement and arousal of buying and selling stocks were intoxicating. Within three years, he had achieved his financial goal and had great successes in a rising market. He began to use cocaine to enhance his feelings of mastery and success.

Because he was in a hurry and felt confident, Anthony started to take larger financial risks, buying futures on margin. His success continued, and he became a rising star in his company. Ultimately he risked too much and lost $50,000 in what was a minor market downturn for others. His cocaine habit became a desperate refuge as he tried to fend off the emotional impact of this catastrophic reality. Anthony had to accept his total defeat before he could start a new life with the help of Gamblers Anonymous and Cocaine Anonymous.

Evaluating Your Escape Risk

You can estimate your risk of becoming compulsive about escapes by examining the risk factors in your life. Use a 2-10 scale to rate each factor, where 2 = very untrue of me, 4 = moderately untrue of me, 6 = slightly true of me, 8 = moderately true of me and 10 = very true of me.

Problem Emotional Adjustments   **Rating**

1. I am troubled by low self-esteem.   _10_
2. Past unresolved emotions are a problem for me.   _10_
3. I have difficulty trusting myself, others and the world.   _6_

Complications of Compulsive Life Patterns

4. I have neglected taking care of myself properly through resting, eating a healthful diet and taking part in regular exercise.   _10_
5. I get sick frequently or have pain and stress-related problems.   _6_
6. Mental health problems, such as depression, anxiety or insomnia, detract from my life.   _10_
7. There are conflicts in my family or marriage that concern me.   _10_
8. Conflicts with co-workers, employers or employees are a problem for me.   _8_
9. I experience symptoms of burnout such as cynicism, apathy or fatigue.   _10_
10. Painful emotions, such as shame, guilt, anger or disappointment, bother me a great deal.   _10_

Personal History with Escapes

11. Members of my family regularly used particular escapes to cope with life while I was growing up.   _10_
12. Members of my family or my relatives have had trouble with compulsive escapes in the past.   _10_
13. I "fell in love" with a certain way of escaping as a teenager or young adult.   _16_

14. My chosen escape did not initially lead to prohib-
    itive consequences.   _6_

    Total   _126_

Your Scores

Your possible score on this survey ranges from 28 to 140. A
total score of 50 or below suggests that you may be at
relatively low risk for becoming compulsive about escapes.
Scores between 50 and 80 suggest moderate risk, and scores
between 80 and 140 suggest very high risk. Even though your
overall score is low, however, you may still be at high risk if
you have a few very high scores or a family history of
compulsive escape behavior. You can take your personal risk
score into account as you make decisions about your escapes
in Chapter 9.

How Escapes Become Compulsive

There are four common phases in the development of
compulsive escapes:

1. We make friends with an escape. Once we learn about
drinking alcohol, taking drugs, eating our favorite foods,
having sex, going on spending sprees, having powerful
religious experiences, taking physical risks or gambling, we
often find that these actions feel good and don't have
immediate unacceptable consequences. Therefore, we repeat
them. We learn over a long period of time that we can count
on our escapes to achieve reliable changes of consciousness
(Johnson, 1973). As we become compulsive about escapes, we
have hundreds or thousands of experiences with those
activities and learn to rely on them to face our lives. We come
to depend on our escapes psychologically and at times
physically. Often minimal initially, the consequences of our
escapes gradually increase to the drastic point.

Hooked On Running

Danielle was ashamed of her parents, who were both overweight. Her childhood resolve was to never allow herself to

become fat. In college, she joined the cross-country team and found that she loved running. She continued running after college and competed frequently in races and marathons.

Her husband was also an athlete and liked to stay in shape, but he did not have Danielle's zeal. He felt that she was overdoing it with her ten-mile daily runs, but Danielle was fascinated with pushing herself to her physical limits. She continued running even though she developed a chronic problem with one knee. If she missed a workout, she became extremely irritable. Her husband felt abandoned and resented the amount of time she was away. They had sex infrequently, partly as a result of Danielle's intensive training, and he resented this as well.

The couple began to try to have a child, but Danielle was unable to conceive. A medical evaluation identified compulsive exercising as a probable factor in her infertility. Even though her running now stood in the way of family harmony and her wish to get pregnant, Danielle found it extremely difficult to slow down. Running had become a compulsive escape for her. Danielle had to let go of her quest for physical perfection to begin recovery.

2. Our problems and pain increase. On top of the problems we faced before we adopted our escape behavior, we create new problems for ourselves with our compulsive escapes. First, we escape instead of acting to solve our day-to-day problems, and second, our escapes eventually lead to new complications.

Flying High

Brent came home from work every day angry about a domineering supervisor. He couldn't stand up to his boss, but he could change his perspective by smoking marijuana. When he was stoned, work issues seemed less important to him, and he could relax and enjoy the evening. On weekends, Brent retreated to his hobby of hang-gliding. Risk-taking became a way for him to reaffirm his manhood even though he couldn't take a stand with his supervisor.

Brent's anger increased until he felt ready to leave his job. His wife was unhappy because he was stoned every night. She resented the time he spent hang-gliding and the unnecessary risks he took by going out on windy days. When she criticized him, Brent often exploded, venting his pent-up frustration about work on her. Brent would not seek help for himself until his wife had already decided to end the marriage.

3. We feel remorse over our actions. As we escape more and more, our actions are neither in our best interests nor consistent with our personal values. We damage our self-respect and create new pain, which we handle with more escaping. Ultimately, we feel unable to stop our escape behavior, even though we know we face significant consequences.

Shopping Into Debt

To comfort herself about not having the boyfriend she wanted, Angela used her credit cards to buy clothes. Her parents had emphasized frugality, but she rebelled against this, telling herself that she needed to be stylish in order to compete professionally and socially. Over a two-year period, her credit-card debts became overwhelming. Even though she earned a good income as a paralegal, she had a hard time making her payments. She resolved over and over to stop spending money until she caught up — but the next time she felt depressed and lonely (and had any new credit available), she went on a shopping spree. Angela had to cut up her credit cards for good and agree to have a trusted friend monitor all her spending to start her recovery.

4. Escaping becomes chronic. As time goes on, we give escapes priority over our personal values, health, relationships and job responsibilities. Health problems, remorse, depression or family conflicts increase until we feel out of control and desperate.

Prisoner Of Sex

Nick's father had had a number of extramarital affairs while Nick was growing up. When Nick learned of these as a teenager, he became very disillusioned. He was angry with his father for betraying his mother and resolved never to do that in his own marriage. At the same time, however, Nick learned covertly that to be masculine was to be a ladies' man.

In college, Nick found that he was quite attractive to women and began to enjoy the challenge of making sexual conquests. His reputation with his male friends was as a womanizer, and he liked his status. He saw himself as "sowing wild oats," but his relationships didn't last because he lost interest soon after the romantic phase of each affair. He began to use pornography as a way to increase his sexual interest.

By his late 20s, Nick had developed the habit of going to massage parlors for sexual release. He also found that sex with prostitutes was much more intense than with his girlfriends. When he contracted herpes from one of his sexual encounters, he was shocked. He realized how important sexuality had become to his self-esteem. He realized that he did not know how to have an enduring relationship, yet he wanted to get married and have a family. Nick's craving for sex had become a trap for him. He required inpatient treatment for his compulsive sexual behavior to interrupt his destructive pattern. He then had to learn how to be intimate in other ways.

Image 8 portrays the crisis point in compulsive escapes, when real problems threaten us with disaster. Four escape patterns are pictured: alcohol abuse, cigarette abuse, compulsive overeating and compulsive sexual behavior (p. 74).

Evaluating Your Escapes

As a first step in recovery, you need to decide which escapes do not fit with your value system and best interests. The following discussion and questionnaire give you some criteria to consider as you evaluate your escapes.

Destructive Escapes

Escapes that are illegal, involve physical risks or have high compulsive potential are not in our best interests. If we use street drugs, patronize prostitutes or take part in other illicit sexual activities, or participate in illegal gambling, we risk legal and health consequences, humiliation and lost self-respect. Binge-and-vomit eating cycles; excessive fasting or extreme diets; death-defying activities such as rock climbing without ropes; ignoring safety procedures in parachuting, kayaking or scuba diving; dangerous driving; and driving while under the influence of alcohol or drugs are all destructive. Cigarette smoking is powerfully linked to ill health and to

Last Supper at the Escape Cafe. *Each cafe patron turns to his or her chosen escape for comfort, momentarily unaware of the looming disaster of real problems that will soon destroy this refuge.*

the suppression of feelings. Some people can smoke on a limited basis without apparent harm, but most of us who begin become compulsive smokers.

If you use any of these destructive escapes, carefully consider the costs you are paying and the risks you run. The following questionnaire will help you determine if any other escapes have become compulsive for you. During recovery, you can replace compulsive escapes, one by one, with positive, self-fulfilling behavior.

Your Use Of Escapes

Use a 2-10 scale for each statement about common escapes, where 2 = very untrue of me, 4 = moderately untrue of me, 6 = slightly true of me, 8 = moderately true of me and 10 = very true of me.

Alcohol Use   Rating
1. I consider alcohol a problem in my life.   *2*
2. I constantly think about or look forward to drinking. *2*
3. I behave in ways that I regret when I drink.   *2*
4. I drink to avoid negative feelings.   *2*
5. I try to change my drinking habits and fail.   *2*

   Total   *10*

Food Use
1. I consider the way I use food a problem.   *10*
2. I constantly think about or look forward to eating.   *10*
3. I overeat frequently and feel guilty.   *10*
4. I eat to avoid negative feelings.   *10*
5. I try to change my eating habits and fail.   *10*

   Total   *50*

Sexual Behavior
1. I consider sex a problem in my life.   *2*
2. I constantly think about or look forward to sex.   *4*
3. I do things sexually that I later regret.   *4*
4. I have sex in order to avoid negative feelings.   *2*

5. I try to change my sexual behavior and fail.   2

Total   14

Exercising
1. I think I exercise compulsively.   2
2. I constantly think about or look forward to exercising.   2
3. I create problems for myself because of my exercising.   2
4. I exercise in order to avoid negative feelings.   2
5. I try to change my exercise behavior and fail.   2

Total   10

Religious Behavior
1. I think I overdo my personal reliance on religious practices.   2
2. I constantly think about or look forward to my religious activities.   2
3. I neglect doing things I need to do because of my religious activities.   2
4. I become involved in religious practice or activity to avoid negative feelings that I need to face.   2
5. I have tried to modify my religious practices in the past and have been unable to do so.   2

Total   10

Spending Money
1. I think I overspend.   2
2. I constantly think about or look forward to spending money.   2
3. I spend money that I later regret spending.   6
4. I spend money in order to avoid negative feelings.   2
5. I try to change my spending habits and fail.   2

Total   14

Gambling (Taking Risks with Money)
1. I think I have a problem with gambling.   2
2. I constantly think about or look forward to gambling.   2

3. I gamble with money I cannot afford to lose.   2
4. I gamble in order to avoid negative feelings.   2
5. I try to change my gambling habits and fail.   2

Total   10

Your Scores

A score of 24 or more for a particular escape pattern or single very high scores imply that you may have become compulsive with that escape.

If you find that you have become compulsive about one or more escapes, you are not alone. Chapters 7 and 8 describe resources for recovery and how to prepare for active recovery. Guidelines for replacing compulsive escapes are presented in Chapter 9. Keep the faith!

7. THE RECOVERY LANDSCAPE

By making it this far, you have demonstrated your willingness to work for the life you want. Effort, courage, time and faith, in human proportions, are all that the remaining steps to recovery require. There is a saying in recovery circles: "You are responsible for the effort, and forces greater than yourself are responsible for the outcome." If you do what you can on a daily basis to improve yourself and your life, you can achieve a personal transformation, even though you control only part of how your life develops.

Our past attempts to change survival patterns usually failed because, unsupported and uninformed, we became discouraged when we confronted a lifetime of habit and emotion. Uninterrupted survival behavior was leading us to disaster — unhappiness, illness or complications from compulsive life patterns and compulsive escapes, or even premature death from despair.

Survival behavior patterns are solutions based on illusion. Ideas such as, "I can find a shortcut," "I can get away with it," "I will win the lottery," "I can find someone to take care of me," or "I can do it by myself," have to go. We have to restructure our attitudes, behavior, beliefs and relationships during recovery, not suddenly or dramatically but as part of a growing process. Growth is sometimes so subtle that we can't detect it. Later we feel the changes happening inside, and ultimately we create different lives for ourselves. Survival patterns are intricate, invisible and powerful. By the time we recognize them and begin to recover, we may have used these strategies thousands of times. It is quite a challenge to change these overlearned patterns, and we need new knowledge, skills and support with which to transform them into strengths. These resources are now available to us. This chapter identifies tasks to accomplish as you recover and describes how you can use self-help groups and holistic psychotherapy for help along the way.

Recovery Tasks

There are eight general tasks to accomplish during recovery. You don't have to do these in a certain order. You will probably work on each task many times at deeper intellectual and emotional levels during recovery. When you complete these tasks you will be able to say, "I am at peace with the past. I feel good about the person I am today and I am excited about my future."

Recovery tasks are:

1. Understand your life process.
2. Take responsibility for yourself.
3. Learn about and feel your emotions.
4. Heal from painful experiences.
5. Identify and stop your unproductive patterns.
6. Discover and practice productive patterns.
7. Learn to prevent new problems.
8. Plan for your future happiness.

The remaining chapters present specific guidelines for you to follow as you complete these tasks.

You might learn something from the following story, which illustrates Barbara's recovery from low self-esteem, victim syndrome and compulsive religious behavior.

Barbara's Recovery

"I am 31 now and feel good about my life. I started recovery three years ago. My husband Bill was depressed about his job, and we weren't getting along. My son was rebelling at home and doing badly in school. During a routine checkup I found out that I had uterine cancer. The cancer was in the early stages and had not spread so that surgery got it all, but it really scared me. I started questioning how I was living. Bill and I had belonged to a religious group, which was almost a cult, since before we got married. What finally happened was that I realized I had to get away from this organization.

"I had felt bad about myself ever since childhood. I was the oldest child in my family and got a lot of attention and affection until I was three. Then my brother was born, and my parents, particularly my father, turned all their attention to him. I see now that I was traumatized by this and felt that there must be something wrong with me. As a child I tried very hard to get my father to love me by doing well in school and other achievements, but he always seemed to favor my brother.

"By the time I went away to college I was pretty depressed. I dated a man my freshman year and had my first sexual experience with him even though I didn't feel completely ready. Shortly after that he left me and started going out with one of my friends. I was humiliated and angry and felt like I didn't belong anywhere. I was drawn to this religious group because I needed people who cared about me and would show me how to live. They accepted me and provided a refuge, which I needed."

Looking For A Father

"The leader of the group was a father figure for me, and I tried to get a lot of the fathering from him that I never got from my father, who was an alcoholic and never close to me. We were taught to submit to the authority of the group in all our decisions. We were discouraged from having contact with people who were not part of our group. At that time I liked the structure and it helped me discipline my life. I loved the singing, sharing, prayer and meditations, and I had moments of deep spiritual awareness.

"Bill joined the group at about the same time as I, and we fell in love with each other during the first year we met. We got married soon after that and I dropped out of school. I was taught to submit to his authority and that my place was at home. My son Kyle was born two years later. I liked being a homemaker when he was little, but I began to feel incomplete after he started school. I had always planned to develop a career for myself. I spent more and more time each day praying, attending services and helping with our religious activities. Deep down I was unhappy. When the cancer was diagnosed I realized that I couldn't go on this way."

Starting To Think For Herself

"I started to question the authority of the leader and the group, and they began to ostracize me. This went on for several months before I realized that I had to leave the group. It was terrifying to me to break out of this community of people I had known so well and gone through a lot with. But there was no middle ground. They could not tolerate my decision to find my own way as a woman and as a wife. Bill was in the middle for a long time, but it finally came down to them or me. He decided to stay with me.

"When I left the group I realized how lost I was. I was hit with a lot of fear and grief, which I had been running from my whole life. I started going to Adult Children of Alcoholics Al-Anon meetings, and that program has really helped me. I had to work out a whole new relationship with Bill, and we saw a counselor together for about a year. We have grown a lot. In the meantime, I started working in a bank and have been promoted twice. I think Bill feels better now because he doesn't have to carry the whole financial burden of the family.

"Over the past two years I have done some good things for myself. I am in good physical shape and I am eating carefully. I found a church that supports my faith but doesn't dictate my personal decisions or deny my autonomy. Kyle seems to be doing a lot better because Bill and I are happier. I think that he was acting out the tension that he sensed in me. I am grateful to be running my own life with the support of my family and friends and with the help of my personal God."

The Self-Help Revolution

In the past, recovery information and self-help groups were not available. People trying to recover sought help from professionals who often didn't understand survival processes and were using limited psychotherapy theories and techniques. As a result, many people did not recover. Fortunately, we now have resources that dramatically improve our chances for success in recovery.

The self-help revolution began with Alcoholics Anonymous. Now, self-help is available for many human problems. If we struggle with compulsive patterns like overeating or gambling, illnesses like cancer or heart disease, losses like divorce or the death of a child, or destructive behavior like child abuse or family violence, we can find guidance, hope and support from others who have faced the same problems.

In self-help groups we learn to make sense of our experiences and gain hope. It is inspiring to see, hear and learn from others as they go through their own recoveries. We learn that we are not bad people because of our problems. For instance, AA shows alcoholics how the dynamics of addiction are more powerful than unaided individuals. This relieves problem drinkers' shame about being "weak" or "immoral," which can often lead to further drinking. Overeaters Anonymous helps its members see that food was a way of coping with feelings they felt they could not face another way. Adult Children of Alcoholics Al-Anon helps people who grew up in alcoholic families see that they are not "sick" or "crazy" but are experiencing normal reactions and adjustments to abnormal situations.

Many self-help groups follow the AA "Twelve Steps," which break recovery down into specific actions to accomplish daily. The steps outline five phases for recovery:

1. Acknowledging and accepting the truth about our difficulties
2. Becoming willing to accept help
3. Learning lessons from the past and acting to change ourselves for the better
4. Righting the harm we have done to ourselves and others to the best of our ability
5. Developing a realistic and satisfying new way of life

Twelve-step groups are spiritually based ways of living. We can define a "Power greater than ourselves" as a resource for dealing with life. People's definitions of *Higher Power* range from viewing the group as a Higher Power or trusting natural laws to accepting a traditional Judeo-Christian definition of God.

Self-help groups teach us that we must take charge of our own recoveries, but we don't have to do it alone. We can ask for help from others, but we supply our own elbow grease. Those of us who grew up in troubled families can receive positive regard and acceptance from our support groups as we gather strength for recovery. We can reduce emotional deprivation and have the choice to never be lonely again. Consider using a self-help group as a resource during your recovery.

Holistic Psychotherapy

Psychotherapy did not exist prior to the twentieth century. Sigmund Freud created the first formal psychological helping relationship with psychoanalysis. Each psychological theory developed since Freud has contributed to our understanding of how whole people work. Each separate theory, however, is not enough to explain and change survival behavior patterns. Holistic psychotherapy integrates major developments from the mental health field, family therapy and study of addictions into the helping process.

The following dimensions of change are essential to helping people recover from survival behavior patterns:

1. Opportunities for new relationship learning. The relationship between psychotherapist and client is the foundation of helpful change. We need to work with helpers who care about us and who are warm and direct. We can learn about successful relationships by solving any conflicts that arise between ourselves and our helpers. Psychotherapy offers a kind of *reparenting* in which we can receive undivided and compassionate attention. This is a healing alternative to our often difficult relationships with our parents.

2. Practice in compassionate self-understanding. As we understand ourselves and are treated with respect in psychotherapy, we learn to treat ourselves in new, strengthening ways. We can understand ourselves more compassionately in terms of family limitations rather than through dehumanizing diagnostic terms like *neurosis* or *personality disorder*, which are equated by most people with being *sick*, *weak* or *bad*. Because we carry on a continual internal dialogue in which we often discount ourselves, exaggerate events, jump to conclusions, personalize or say harsh things to ourselves, we need help to become aware of and change our critical self-statements into realistic and supportive internal messages (Burns, 1980).

3. Direct problem solving and new skill development. Survival behavior patterns are usually invisible to those of us who are caught up in them. We need clear explanations and direct feedback about what we can do. For instance, a person addicted to alcohol needs to hear directly that drinking is threatening his or her health and safety, is driving loved ones away, and that it would be in his or her best interests to stop drinking. Self-understanding alone does not lead to behavior change. We need support and careful teaching as we develop and practice new, more effective skills. For example, to recover, an alcoholic needs to learn ways to relax without drinking, how to express painful feelings and ways to build genuine self-respect and self-esteem.

4. Support in facing painful life experiences. Feelings of grief, anger, hurt, disappointment and shame arise as we remember and recount painful events during recovery. We require safety and understanding in order to face these feelings and move on. Powerful emotions also develop as we come to new realizations or decisions during recovery. For instance, we may recognize that we never felt safe and secure as children and experience grief about not having the chance to be carefree and innocent. As we give up compulsive escapes, we may feel angry that the actions that provided solace or fun to us are no longer available.

5. Encouragement for self-responsibility and self-care. Growth during recovery is directly proportional to the efforts we make. We need encouragement and guidance in taking responsibility for ourselves. We need direction toward specific tasks that will assist our learning process. We must learn positive self-care skills, including nutrition, exercise, health care, recreation, relaxation and spiritual self-development.

6. Experiential learning and healing approaches. Verbal techniques alone are insufficient for people who have experienced significant trauma. Approaches to experiential learning and healing, such as gestalt psychotherapy, psychodrama, family sculpture, hypnosis, therapeutic massage and imagery, help us bypass the "paralysis of analysis" and gain awareness of our bodies and our feelings. These active psychotherapies allow learning and feeling through action, movement and touch.

Considering Professional Help

Throughout this book, you have completed several self-assessments of your well-being, including "Your Basic Human Needs" and "Evaluating Your Childhood Circumstances" in Chapter 2, "Your Self-Esteem" and "Your Unresolved Emotions" in Chapter 4, the compulsive life pattern self-assessments in Chapter 5, and "Evaluating Your Escape Risk" and "Your Use of Escapes" in Chapter 6. If your childhood needs were very frustrated, your family had significant problem characteristics, you feel out of control with compulsive life patterns, you are at high risk for escapes, or you have developed compulsive escapes, you may need professional help during recovery.

If you have faced your life alone in the past, consider giving yourself compassionate support. You do not have to be in deep trouble to benefit from the help of another person, but certain symptoms do suggest a definite need for professional help: (1) suicidal feelings or actions, (2) prolonged depression or anxiety, (3) violent or aggressive behavior, and (4) health complications. Use your best judgment in deciding when to seek help and what help is right for you.

You Are Responsible

We may bring with us from childhood the illusion that we can find someone who will take care of us. The truth of adult life is that we can find others who only will help us along the way. If we surrender our responsibility for ourselves, we are often victimized. The only exceptions to this are those moments in life when we are so weak, sick or vulnerable that we must rely on the compassion and good intentions of others. For the rest of the time, the other people in our lives are there only to consult with — and we pay the price if their advice is wrong. None of our "consultants" wish for anything bad to happen to us, but if it does, *we* are responsible. We need to find the best consultants we can, yet make our own final decisions.

Image 9 illustrates this principle (p. 88).

James' Therapist Change

James felt that he was not making progress with the therapist he had been seeing for two years. He felt more depressed than ever. His therapist was not trained in understanding family systems and seemed to view James' case as hopeless. When James joined a self-help group for adults from troubled families, his therapist did not really support the move. After James learned about survival behavior patterns, he decided to find a helper who had specific training and understanding in recovery techniques.

Your Commitment To Recovery

Personal recovery does not mean "as good as new." It means we become happier, freer, wiser, more productive, more grateful and more humble, even while carrying the scars and memories of painful times and painful choices. Review in your mind all that you have been through so far. Remember the personal courage, determination and toughness you have mustered in order to survive the challenges you have faced. And remember the people who have made a difference in your life along the way by believing in you or by bestowing kindness. You can achieve the deep satisfaction that comes from living according to your values. There are many people out there who can help and support you along the way.

Fly By Your Own Instruments. *Flying a small plane in the midst of a threatening storm represents the difficult parts of our journey through life. Winds, thunderheads and jagged peaks can destroy us in our fragile machine if we do not use all of our wisdom and skill to maneuver our way through to the clear skies on the other side. We can consult by radio with advisors on how to proceed, but only by reading our own instruments, making our best judgments and using all of our skill do we ultimately get through. Please fly by your own instruments!*

8. GETTING IN SHAPE

It is time to commit to a training program for recovery! You began your recovery when you acknowledged that something was wrong with your life. You have gathered new information from this book and other sources. You probably recognize yourself in some of the survival patterns described. Understanding and facing these patterns is a tremendous step forward. Now you need to get into shape so that you can join the many people who are looking for and finding ways of life that are balanced and satisfying, free of compulsive patterns. You, too, can achieve freedom!

You may recall the stages of behavior change discussed in Chapter 1: recognition, hope, clarity, preparation, action and continuation. You have already made progress with recognition, hope and clarity. Now is the time for preparation. During preparation, we muster the strength we need to transform life-long survival patterns into freedom lifestyles. Like athletes training for a 10-K run, we work to improve our form and make choices that increase our stamina for the upcoming challenge. You can begin your conditioning by starting the recovery processes described in this chapter: "Caring For Your Inner Child" and "Designing A Personal Recovery Plan." Once you have these under way, you will be ready to carry out the transformation tasks described in Chapters 9, 10 and 11.

Caring For Your Inner Child

Eric Berne described the inner self as having parent, adult and child parts (cited in Woolams and Brown, 1979). Our *parent* self refers to our capacity to evaluate positively or negatively. Our *adult* self refers to our knowledge, competence and ability to solve problems. Our *child* self includes feelings, intuition, creativity, humor, spontaneity, sexuality and spirituality. During recovery, we expand beyond the limits of the childhood selves we developed as we broaden our values; develop new understanding and skills; and discover feelings, intuition and creative potential.

In this book, you have evaluated your life in new ways and developed new understanding. You have learned that your family of childhood met certain needs but didn't provide other crucial elements for your well-being. The deprived, hurt, rejected, ashamed, frightened, sad or lonely boy or girl of your childhood remains with you. Negative feelings block your positive possibilities. To allow healing, you can "reparent" your child-self during recovery (Whitfield, 1987). Put special effort into providing the things you missed while growing up. As you care for the little boy or girl within you, your child-self will give you in return energy, spontaneity, creativity, spirituality and fun with which to transform your life into a joyful and worthwhile experience. The following recovery tools will help you build strength and begin to overcome low self-esteem.

Gentle Words For Yourself

You may still speak to yourself internally in the same harsh way that you were spoken to as a child. This perpetuates painful childhood feelings and low self-esteem. Be careful about what you say to yourself during your recovery. Your child-self believes what you say whether it is true or not. If you say degrading, critical or frightening things to yourself, you will feel ashamed, inadequate or scared. When you substitute forgiving, encouraging and hopeful internal dialogue, you begin to feel lovable, competent and brave. Catch yourself if you say harsh things and try to say something compassionate instead, such as, "I didn't know how to do it differently. I am learning through experience, and I am trying out some new options as best as I can."

Your Self-Care Plan

What do you need to do to start feeling better about yourself? Set some self-care goals to strive toward at your own pace. Do not expect yourself to accomplish these goals immediately or perfectly. They are merely guidelines to keep in mind and accomplish as you are able.

Your next task is to list activities in each of the following areas that you would like to do for yourself on a daily or weekly basis.

1. Physical health care (including diet, exercise, rest and medical, dental or other professional care)
2. Emotional well-being (including self-help groups, workshops, journal writing or psychotherapy)
3. Spiritual well-being (including reading, meditation, prayer, church attendance or communing with nature)
4. Intimate relationships (daily or weekly time set aside for family members and close friends)
5. Meaning and accomplishment (long-term goals and aims in both your work and personal life that will provide a sense of excitement and direction in your daily life)
6. Recreation and fun (laughter, playing, being out in nature or any other nonproblem-solving activity)

Reread your self-care plan regularly. Set some general time goals so that you can check your progress; but, be forgiving if it takes somewhat longer than you expected. Most of us spend several years working toward achieving these goals. Update your plan as you need to.

Designing A Personal Recovery Plan

All successful projects begin with a clear picture of the present situation and a vision of a future creation. A summary of your findings about your life patterns so far will give you a baseline against which to measure your progress. Then you can design exactly how you want things to be instead.

Your Recovery Plan

All of the problem emotional adjustments, compulsive behavior patterns and complications discussed so far are listed below. On a separate sheet of paper, note each pattern and complication that applies to you. Below each characteristic, write a one-paragraph description of how that pattern appears in your life now. This is a snapshot of your "survival" pattern.

On the same sheet, below each pattern you have described, write down a pattern of living with which you will replace the old pattern over time, even if you don't know now exactly how you will accomplish this. This is a snapshot of your "freedom" pattern. Charles' recovery plan, which follows the list of survival patterns and complications, provides an example.

This exercise requires effort and thought and may take several days to complete. Remember that a written personal plan can be extremely important to your recovery. Writing things down is a powerful tool for change. Once you develop your plan, you will find it to be a helpful reminder to make choices that further your recovery.

Survival Patterns And Complications

Problem Emotional Adjustments
  having low self-esteem
  having unresolved emotions
  having difficulty in trusting

Compulsive Life Patterns
  working compulsively
  displaying relationship dependency
  displaying generalized rebellion
  manifesting victim syndrome
  manifesting perpetual-child syndrome

Complications of Compulsive Life Patterns
  neglecting self-care, diet and exercise
  having health problems
  having mental health problems, such as
    depression
    anxiety
    insomnia
  experiencing family or marital conflict
  experiencing conflict at work

experiencing burnout symptoms, such as
cynicism
fatigue
apathy
having painful feelings, such as
shame
guilt
helplessness
anger
disappointment

Compulsive Escapes
overeating and vomiting
fasting or extreme dieting
overeating compulsively
participating in death-defying activities
abusing street drugs
smoking cigarettes
abusing alcohol
abusing prescription drugs
indulging in compulsive sexual behavior
exercising compulsively
spending compulsively
engaging in compulsive religious behavior
taking excessive risks with money or gambling

Complications of Compulsive Escapes
having health problems
experiencing relationship conflict
having conflict at work
having painful feelings

Charles' Recovery Plan

Charles became depressed after he lost his job as a sales representative. He was worried about his career, his marriage and his drinking. The four problems he wished to replace with freedom patterns are: (1) low self-esteem, (2) unresolved emotions, (3) victim syndrome, and (4) alcohol abuse.

Low Self-Esteem

"I feel like a failure because I just lost my job. I spend so much time down and doubting myself that I can't get organized to look for work, and I don't have any energy. I am doing something seriously wrong in my life. I'm not making much of a difference or contribution to the world. I don't think I deserve my wife's love. I feel like I am getting away with something because someone like her believes in me. When she figures out I am a failure she will leave me."

Goal: High Self-Esteem

"I like where I am in my life, what I am doing and who I am with. I trust myself and if something goes wrong, I know that I have done my best and don't have to blame myself. I deserve to be with someone as special as my wife, and I accept her respect for me. I have found a satisfying job that allows me to express my talents. I have energy and enthusiasm for life. I contribute to the world by being decent, straightforward and positive with people."

Unresolved Emotions

"I have felt lonely and angry and sad off and on since my parents got divorced when I was 12. That was really a hard time for me. I knew they weren't getting along, but I wanted them to stay together. My mother kicked my dad out because he wasn't taking responsibility for the family. He didn't work regularly and she mostly supported us. I felt ashamed because we were in a small town and everyone knew my parents were divorced.

"Before the divorce, my dad did a lot of things with me like fishing and camping. After they got divorced, he moved away and I didn't see him nearly as much. He felt that I was on Mom's side because I chose to live with her. I haven't been close to him since, and this really hurts me. I haven't ever talked about my feelings to either one of them."

Goal: Feeling At Peace With The Past

"I realize that my parents' divorce paralyzed me as a kid because I felt abandoned by my dad and ashamed because my family was falling apart. I no longer feel responsible for their choices. I understand that their divorce had nothing to do with me. I have expressed my hurt about what happened and am ready to move on. I know that what I felt is what other children go through in divorced families. I want to talk to both of my parents about what happened to see if I can start new relationships with them."

Victim Syndrome

"I don't seem to know what is right for me. I thought my new job was what I wanted, but I lost it because my boss expected me to develop my market area more quickly than I realistically could. I heard from friends before I took the position that he was impossible to please, but I needed a job and was afraid nothing else would turn up. As I look back I was naive to think that it would work out."

Goal: Self-Responsibility

"I know myself and what kind of work situation is right for me. I know that in really demanding and critical environments I don't do my best so I will avoid those environments. I am learning what I need to do professionally and realize I can find out certain things only through experience. I trust my way of selling, which is to build relationships with people who have an interest in my product rather than to spend a lot of time on people who are not ready or interested. I will hold out for a position that is right for me even though it is frightening to be unemployed."

Alcohol Abuse

"I have several beers after work most days and then watch TV and get nothing accomplished all evening. On weekends I start drinking beer while I do chores in the morning and then have a beer open for the rest of the day. By late afternoon I am pretty high. My wife is unhappy about this because I don't want to do anything in the evening or am too drunk to go out. Sunday I start drinking beer while I watch football and end up wasting the whole day because I don't have any energy, or I just go on drinking until I am sloshed. By Monday morning I feel bad physically and know that I threw away a lot of time I could have used to get things accomplished."

Goal: Non-Drinking Lifestyle

"I am at risk of becoming an alcoholic. My grandfather was an alcoholic and I probably have some genetic risk. I will find

ways to feel good about myself and my life without drinking.
I know that if I drink at all I end up overdoing it. I want to join
a health club and exercise in the late afternoons to get in shape.
Then I will be able to do something constructive in the
evening like read, work in my shop or spend time with my
wife and feel good about myself. On weekends, I know that I
can work efficiently. I want to finish fixing the motorcycle I
am rebuilding and take some road trips. I want to do things
socially with my wife without being out of it."

Like Charles, you can design a recovery plan for yourself. It
will serve you well! With your self-care plan and personal
recovery plan in place, you are ready for the obstacle course.

Image 10 portrays this moment (p. 97).

Pinnacle of Peace: Health Fulfillment

Cliff of Spiritual Growth

River of Bad Relationships

Quicksand of Addiction

Ready for the Obstacle Course. *With appropriate help, training and conditioning, you are now fully prepared to enter the obstacle course of recovery. The course involves some difficult terrain and natural hazards, but the satisfaction of achieving the ultimate goal justifies the risks. Go for it!*

9. ON THE PATH TO FREEDOM

What did you really want and need when you developed your survival patterns? You needed things like stability, affection, protection and support. During recovery, you can find constructive ways to give these things to yourself, maybe for the first time. You can be thankful that you found even compulsive ways of making it through your difficulties, but now, through recovery, you have new options. The next three chapters give you a transformation map to follow on the path to freedom. This chapter describes how to replace compulsive escapes. Chapter 10 describes how to change compulsive patterns, and Chapter 11 discusses the process of continuing to overcome problem emotional adjustments and maintain your recovery.

The Transformation Process

Devote your energy to one priority at a time during recovery. We normally confront compulsive escapes early in the process because these patterns threaten our self-esteem, health and safety. After confronting escapes, we probably need to change our compulsive patterns because these also can create significant complications. As we eliminate our compulsive patterns, we gain the confidence to overcome our re-

maining problem emotional adjustments. Sometimes, however, we have to deal with childhood feelings before we can
replace an escape or life pattern. We need to always "fly by
our own instruments," deciding what makes sense for us at a
given moment. Progress in one survival area strengthens and
prepares us for growth in another.

Replacing Compulsive Escapes

We may say, "I just want to be happy." Unfortunately, our
search for pure happiness through escapes was leading instead
to disaster. Many recovering people regard their years of
pursuing compulsive escapes as an expression of "misguided
spiritual yearning." Age-old spiritual wisdom about the true
path to happiness can be summarized in four guidelines for
daily living:

1. Be thankful that you are alive.
2. Live your life the best way you can, being true to what
   you feel is right.
3. Take care of and care about yourself and show caring
   to others.
4. Make the contributions to your family and community
   that you can, using the talents that you have.

These guidelines outline the essence of a recovery lifestyle.
Because compulsive escapes directly threaten our ability to
live by these principles, we need to establish *personal escape
limits* so that our escapes do not continue to undermine our
well-being.

Personal Escape Limits

For most of us, establishing personal escape limits means
stopping our compulsive escape patterns for good. We cannot
safely continue escape behavior that has become compulsive.
This is true for two reasons: (1) by the time an escape becomes
compulsive, we have exhausted its life-enhancement value;
and (2) we can rarely reestablish a moderate reliance on an
escape that has become compulsive. (Your personal risk score
for compulsive escapes lets you decide if you may be an
exception to this.)

Alcohol or drug abusers often find it necessary to abstain permanently from all mood-altering substances. People who compulsively eat desserts or fatty foods may learn that their personal limit is to eat no foods in these categories under any circumstances. Compulsive spenders may decide in recovery that they must buy nothing on credit. People who use pornography, compulsively masturbate or have sexual affairs often decide that recovery means having sex only with a committed partner.

Your Escape History

To clarify the facts of your escapes, write a history of your experience with each escape that troubles you. (You may want to use Charles' recovery plan for alcohol abuse in Chapter 8 as a model.)

1. Describe your experience with each escape up to the present, beginning with your first memory of using it. In what ways and how frequently have you used the escape (look at time periods of about three months)?
2. What problems in your life have been associated with each escape? How did that escape affect your moods? Did you do things that harmed your health, self-esteem, finances, relationships or job (be specific)?
3. What are the costs and benefits of each escape in your life now? How do you feel after escaping? Is it worth it?
4. What personal escape limits make sense for you?

Living With Your Personal Limits

The time is never "just right" to go through the discomfort of facing life without a convenient anesthetic. Today is as good a day as any to face the world with full consciousness! Take on compulsive escapes one at a time, starting with the escape that is most powerful for you. Others will be easier to replace after you have taken on "the big one." Replacing compulsive escapes means deciding *one by one* not to act on your escape desires. These desires pass within a short period of time if you do something else instead. Drink some fruit juice, take a walk, call a friend or go work out. Take care of yourself physically, mentally and spiritually using your self-care plan. Recovery programs teach "HALT" — never get too hungry, angry, lonely or tired. You are most vulnerable to compulsive escapes when you are in a weakened state. You can break your habit pattern by making 50 to 100 pro-recovery decisions over a period of time. You *can* live within your personal limits.

Desires to escape will come up in circumstances in which you relied on those escapes in the past. An overeater will be tantalized by the wish for cake and ice cream at a birthday party. A problem drinker might envision "a quiet bottle of wine with dinner." A person with a sexual compulsion might fantasize about a "one-night stand" while away from home on business.

Resisting The Urge To Drink

Clint stopped drinking without great difficulty during the last nine months of a three-year product development project. At the project's end, he suddenly had a powerful urge to get drunk with his former drinking companions, a reward he had used in the past for sticking to difficult tasks. He was able to resist this urge because his written escape history revealed that drinking was ruining his marriage. The power of the desire, however, caused him to realize that he had underestimated the power of his dependence on alcohol, and he made the decision that he needed to be part of AA.

Compulsive escapes offer the illusion of making things better. Recovery knowledge allows you to make new choices in situations where your choices were absent or invisible to you before. Absolute clarity about the truth of an escape in your life is the best inoculation against the temptation to return to it. You need to develop stark mental images of your escape choices to help you keep your recovery priorities clear.

Image 11 portrays the knowledge versus illusion choice for a problem drinker (p. 103).

When you replace a compulsive escape, you adopt a new identity that sets you apart from many others. As you live within your limits, you will notice many other people who do not — and they all seem to be getting away with it! Later you

Look Through the Bottom of the Glass. *An attractive lounge beckons the drinker, promising relaxation, sophistication, companionship and fun. The final truth of the evening is humiliation, degradation, embarrassment and sickness, as the drinker embraces his loyal friend, the commode.*

become aware of people who eat carefully and drink carefully or not at all, who no longer smoke and who are loyal in their sexual relationships. You will remember that anticipating an escape, carrying it out, enduring the physical consequences and feeling bad about yourself took a great deal of energy. Freeing yourself from all that is a great accomplishment. Your time and effort are now available to devote to things you couldn't get done before.

Without the anesthetic of escape, you will probably begin to be more aware of the costs of your compulsive life patterns and problem emotional adjustments. You will want to devote some of your new energy and confidence to changing these survival patterns.

10. CHANGING OUR LIFE PATTERNS

Compulsive life patterns started with our childhood attempts to obtain love in troubled families. We needed parental love in the forms of recognition, affection, autonomy, attention and accountability. If we become compulsive workers, we probably needed parental recognition. Those of us with relationship dependency often needed affection and security. If we developed generalized rebellion, we usually needed respect for our personal autonomy. Those of us who become victims needed compassionate parental attention and teaching. If we developed perpetual-child syndrome, we usually needed accountability and encouragement to grow up. You may have needed some or all of these forms of love.

Our childhood attempts to meet our needs were only partially successful because our parents were often poorly prepared for the job of parenting. They were usually caught up in their own survival patterns without the information and resources needed to overcome them. We, however, do have the information and resources we need to change our compulsive life patterns.

Changing our life patterns involves two phases:

1. **Understanding our patterns.** We study our compulsive patterns until we are clear that they don't work in our lives.

2. **Developing recovery patterns.** We define guidelines
   to regulate our compulsive behavior patterns; we
   substitute new information for our unrealistic beliefs;
   and we acquire new skills with which to meet our
   needs.

Understanding Compulsive Life Patterns

Our compulsive strategies usually fail to achieve our goals in
relationships and at work. We may have done our part in our
families of childhood, but others didn't do what we expected.
We then tried to change them but were powerless to do so. As
a result, we brought our expectations and our sense of
powerlessness to adult relationships and work situations or
repeatedly chose relationships and work environments that
did not work out. In this way, we continually replayed our
childhood themes. By completing the following "Personal
Process Inventory," we can examine our life patterns to clarify
what we want and to see where we went off the track. Read
the inventory and the example to understand how it is
organized, and then write about your process.

Personal Process Inventory

1. How did you want things to be in your family during
   childhood and adolescence, in one significant romantic relationship or marriage, and in one work situation?
2. What was your "job description" or expectation for
   yourself in each situation? Did you meet these
   expectations?
3. What was your "job description" or expectation for
   other central people in each situation? Did they meet
   these expectations?
4. If you did not carry out your part in a relationship or
   work situation, what happened then? Did you change
   your behavior, defend yourself, counterattack, try to
   conceal your failure or leave the situation?
5. If other people did not carry out their parts in a
   relationship or work situation, what happened then?
   Did you try to make them do what you expected by
   trying harder at your job, reasoning with them, com-

plaining, withdrawing emotionally, being angry or being self-destructive? Did they change?

6. What happened to your happiness, health, self-esteem, use of escapes, satisfaction and spirituality in each situation?

Fighting For Her Needs

Katherine was a physician who faced problem emotional adjustments, relationship dependency, generalized rebellion and alcohol abuse during recovery.

In Her Family

"In childhood I wanted a happy family, parents who got along, a mother who did not drink and was good to me, a father who respected me and spent time with me, no fighting, fun activities together, everyone loving each other. My job was to be a good kid, do my chores, do well in school, stay out of trouble, be reasonably nice to others. I did these things. My parents' jobs were to love each other, love us, enjoy spending time with the family, not be depressed, not drink and get help if they needed it. They didn't do any of these things.

"To try to change things, I counseled my parents, supported them individually, confronted my mother's drinking, tried to get my father to treat her better, asked him to spend more time with me, pulled back from them, rebelled, got angry, started drinking. Nothing I did made things better.

"I have ended up depressed and angry about my family. I'm ashamed of them and don't like going home. I wish that I didn't come from this family. I'm having a lot of emotional problems that go back to them."

With Her Boyfriend

"I want Rick to be in love with me, to commit to me and plan a life together, to share activities, to accept me. My job is to care about him, do what I say I am going to do, be loyal, be fun to be with, express affection, not overdo drinking. I do these things, except he objects to any drinking. He does not want to see me exclusively or be with me every weekend, does not accept my drinking, and criticizes me and my family.

"I have tried to show Rick that I am a good person. I do things that he wants to do. I am kind to him. I have begged him to commit to me. I have slowed down my drinking. He doesn't want a long-term relationship, so I have pulled back. I feel insecure and angry with him. I don't respect myself because I can't seem to just let go of him. The whole thing depresses me and I drink more even though he objects to it."

At Work

"At the clinic where I work, I want support for the research I have proposed. I want a warm emotional climate for patients, and I want to move toward a more holistic model of treatment. My job is to deliver good patient care, continue learning, develop research ideas and do my best to create a healing climate for patients. I do these things. The administration's job is to improve patient care, welcome new ideas from staff, support research, and support a healing climate. They do not do these things to the extent I think they should.

"I have pushed my research proposal, written memos, talked to administrators, argued in staff meetings and distributed articles on holistic medicine. I haven't had the impact I want to there. Some people at work would like me to leave. I am labeled a troublemaker. I feel bad about it."

Katherine failed to create the family relationships, romantic relationship and work environment that she needed. Her efforts to change other people and systems led to more pain, which she handled with drinking. Her recovery challenge was to find successful ways to meet her needs for affection, recognition and encouragement.

What is your personal process? Do you understand that your compulsive life patterns are not working in your life? When you are ready, return to the "Personal Process Inventory" and write about your own life strategies.

Developing Recovery Patterns

To recover, we need *personal policies* to regulate our compulsive strategies, new information and experience to correct our mistaken beliefs and new skills to balance our lives. Suggested personal policies, realistic beliefs and skills to develop to advance recovery are discussed below. Then the recoveries of five people are described (these peoples' lives illustrated compulsive life patterns in Chapter 5).

Compulsive Working

1. I work or plan for work no more than 50 hours per week.
2. I am broadening my identity by developing new dimensions of myself including recreation, service to others, relationships and spirituality.
3. Every week I plan time to spend with family and friends.
4. I have developed and am putting into action a self-care plan that includes diet, exercise and rest.
5. I recognize and accept that professional success alone does not lead to fulfillment in life.
6. I am learning how to relax during unstructured time.
7. I am learning how to express my feelings and be close to others.

Letting Go Of Work

Todd did not seriously change his compulsive working until he was separated from his wife for several months. Initially, he enjoyed living alone because he could work to his heart's content, but soon he felt empty and lonely even though he was accomplishing a lot. Todd recognized that his open-ended ambition was not leading to fulfillment. He set an income goal that would provide for a reasonable family lifestyle and decided that he could achieve this by working 50 hours per week. This left him with more free time, which he spent with his wife and children. He stopped smoking and reduced his drinking. He began to get into shape and rediscovered skiing and hiking, which he had enjoyed when he was younger. He educated himself about relationships through self-help groups, reading and workshops. When he returned to his wife, he had developed the skills to start a new relationship with her.

Relationship Dependency

1. I invest my time, energy and affection in people who invest equally in me.

2. I honor my wishes, needs and values in my relationships with other adults.
3. I take responsibility for only my part in what goes wrong in my relationships.
4. I try to let other people worry about themselves.
5. I can't make anyone care about me. If I encounter someone who doesn't care about me, I do what I can to find another relationship.
6. I am becoming aware of my feelings and needs in both personal and professional situations.
7. I am learning to protect myself from unfair criticism or abuse.

Finding A New Support System

Rebecca recognized over the course of a year that her marriage could never provide an environment in which she could thrive. Her husband consistently refused to become involved in marital counseling. Rebecca was frightened of confronting life with the financial insecurity and of life without the emotional attention that her husband provided, but after a lot of preparation, she filed for divorce, started graduate school in social work and moved out on her own. She began to feel better about herself almost immediately. She began to take care of her health and lose weight. As a result, she had more energy and enthusiasm than she had had in years.

This initial high faded after a few months, however, and she began to periodically feel fearful and lonely. She started attending Co-dependents Anonymous meetings and for the first time began to seek and find friends who were enthusiastic about who she was. With their support, she could face the financial changes and uncertainty of life on her own. Rebecca became involved two years later with a man who gave her some of the warmth and respect she had always wanted.

Image 12 portrays our capacity to use our adult power to protect our vulnerable child-selves from abuse or mistreatment (p. 111).

Generalized Rebellion

1. I identify my personal and professional responsibilities and try to do the best job I can at meeting them.

The Mother Lion. *A mother lion models how we need to protect and provide for our vulnerable and innocent child-selves. Her cub is always under her watchful eye, and she is prepared to use teeth and claws to protect her offspring from any threat in the environment.*

2. I do not have to be the "heavy" in most situations.
3. I am not responsible for changing what is wrong with other people or organizations. I evaluate each situation according to whether my attempts to help will make things better or worse.
4. If I find myself becoming angry about something, I use this as a cue that I may be taking on a fight that I am powerless to win.
5. I focus my efforts on those things that I have the power to change because there are many things that I can do nothing about.
6. I try to let issues pass without challenge if they are not really my business.
7. I am finding people who can support me in letting go of things that I can't change.

Ending The Campaign

Joseph's extreme anger about work finally led his wife to insist that he get help. He began to attend self-help groups for adults from dysfunctional families. A friend there told him, "You don't have to save the world, just don't make things worse!" This shocked Joseph, and he recognized that his continual campaigning was becoming destructive. He recognized that his reform movements began with his attempts to change his family as a child.

Joseph found it necessary to let go of his resentment about what had gone wrong during his childhood. As he released his hurt and anger about his troubled family, he was able to stop struggling so hard to change his co-workers. He ultimately decided to seek employment with an organization that he did not feel compelled to reform.

Victim Syndrome

1. Whenever possible, I clearly communicate my wants and needs to others in situations that affect my well-being.
2. I know that I cannot rely on anyone to take care of me in my adult life.
3. I do not count on other people to know and understand when I am angry or unhappy unless I tell them directly.

4. I accept that all others in my life are only "consultants" about how to live my life. I make the final decisions for myself.
5. I can't trust everyone, and I am learning to recognize and avoid people who are not reliable.
6. I am learning about my feelings and needs in both personal and professional situations.
7. I am learning to protect myself from unfair criticism or abuse.

Providing For Herself

Lynn was in a financial trap with four children and few career skills. In desperation, she entered psychotherapy at a reduced fee through a pastoral center. To learn to solve her problems, Lynn needed the encouragement and direction she had missed as a child. Through therapy and the support of her church, Lynn began to let go of the fantasy that she would find someone to rescue her. It was painful for her to come to terms with the fact that she had to provide for herself. Lynn took assertiveness training and began to stand up for herself with her children and with other adults. She obtained grant assistance to complete training for secretarial work and word processing. Over a two-year period, she learned to look out for herself and started to build security and stability for herself and her family.

Perpetual-Child Syndrome

1. I do what I say I am going to do.
2. I take responsibility for myself.
3. I do not request that greater allowances be made for me than for others.
4. If someone gets angry at me, I examine whether or not I have provoked this reaction through irresponsibility.
5. I accept that my interests and my self-esteem are being harmed if I feel I am "getting away with something."
6. I understand that life has to be a balance of effort and rest. Very little of value is achieved without hard work over a period of time.

Accountable At Last

Derek's wife began attending a self-help group for spouses

of people with compulsive sexual behavior. She soon told him
that she had decided to end the marriage if Derek did not stop
his affair and give her control over his business spending.
Derek was determined to save his marriage and business, so he
accepted these conditions. He needed someone who would
hold him completely accountable for his behavior. Because his
wife was able to do this, both his marriage and business
survived. Derek recognized that he could not afford to have
people close to him who would let him get away with
perpetual-child behavior. He began to experience genuine
self-respect as he took responsibility for his life.

Your Recovery Guidelines

Which policies, beliefs and skills do you need to guide your
recovery from compulsive strategies? Write them down,
apply them at your own pace and make adjustments as you
need to. As you reduce problems from compulsive life
patterns in your daily life, you are ready to begin the last phase
of recovery.

11. TRANSCENDING TROUBLED FAMILIES

Recovery goes on for life, but we don't always have to work so hard. A time comes during recovery when we realize that we are living different lives — freer, happier and more fulfilling than before. We see that we have gone beyond the limits of our childhoods and that we have become the masters of ourselves, excited about our future possibilities. We see that the way things happened along the way caused us to grow, change and learn. Some people in recovery say that they feel grateful for the way their lives developed because their problems led to the growing process of recovery.

Still, our work is not done. Problem emotional adjustments continue to detract from the quality of our lives. We usually cannot completely replace compulsive escapes and change our compulsive life patterns until we face and overcome unresolved childhood emotions. First, however, we need to slow down or stop the creation of new problems in order to develop the self-awareness, strength and focus necessary to face the past. This chapter describes the emotional healing process and suggests ways to maintain hard-won recovery gains in our lives.

Building Self-Esteem

Our self-esteem steadily increases as we care for our inner child, replace compulsive escapes and change our life patterns. Our progress on these tasks translates readily into self-respect because we are beginning to live a life that is consistent with our values. Rather than starting each day with remorse, shame or fear, we wake up feeling good because we did little yesterday that we regret and a few things that we feel proud of. We don't expect 100 percent improvement, but we do acknowledge and celebrate our growth.

When we put forth our best effort, we can accept our individual rate of change. If our growth at a given moment seems slower than someone else's, this may mean that we had more to overcome or that we endured greater deprivation or trauma. We all have our own struggles. As we attend self-help meetings and learn more about other people's lives, we understand the following AA statement: "We thought we could find an easier, softer, way. But we could not. With all the earnestness at our command, we beg of you to be fearless and thorough from the very start. Some of us have tried to hold on to our old ideas and the result was nil until we let go absolutely" (Alcoholics Anonymous, 1976). To appreciate the changes we are making, we compare ourselves to our own pasts. We can look back at our personal recovery plans from time to time to see how we have grown.

Low self-esteem was often a necessary childhood defense against hurt or disappointment. We no longer have to brace ourselves for the worst by putting ourselves down and feeling unworthy. We discover that our greatest trials are now becoming sources of wisdom and strength. Our growing capacity to be who we are and be honest about the truth of our lives powerfully affects our relationships with family members, friends, employers and employees. People respond to our compassionate honesty with trust and confide in us because they feel safe, and indeed, we have new personal wisdom to share. We gradually make the transition from humiliation to humility. Humiliation is the person-destroying experience of unworthiness, failure and shame. Humility is honest self-respect that incorporates the knowledge of having made mistakes in life but having learned from them, forgiven ourselves and gone on.

Healing Unresolved Emotions

Healing involves facing sometimes overwhelming emotional memories from childhood. As we reexperience in the present how we felt then, we need the help, support and recovery guidance from other people who know the way. Childhood consciousness can arise suddenly and powerfully. For example, if we encounter authority figures who give us negative feedback, we suddenly plunge into profound feelings of shame, humiliation and vulnerability, feelings from long-forgotten childhood moments. Part of the challenge of emotional recovery is that we often don't realize what is happening to us, and the experience feels endless. Our past brief experiences of childhood pain drove us repeatedly back into compulsive patterns. We fear we won't survive our pain. We must remember a recovery saying, "This too shall pass."

When we hurt, our survival instinct is often to push other people away, but we cannot heal alone. Surrendering to our emotions in the presence of loving and supportive people is one of the most transforming experiences of life. When we take risks with safe people (in support groups, for example), we can receive the unconditional positive regard that we have needed for so long, and we begin to experience tenderness, forgiveness, peace, love and joy. We learn that it is impossible to look good and recover at the same time. Some of the emotional "places" we may visit along the way to recovery are listed below. Remember, these are necessary steps along the path to freedom:

> "can't stop crying"
> "ticking time bomb"
> "in a black hole"
> "swimming through molasses"
> "bananas"
> "caught in quicksand"

But sooner or later we arrive at:

> "sitting on top of the world"
> "in love with life"
> "grateful"

Real Feelings Versus Racket Feelings

We learned in our families that certain kinds of negative feelings were all right and others were unacceptable. We then practiced the kinds of negative feelings that were modeled in our homes (Goulding and Goulding, 1979). We translated many of our own negative feelings into the "correct" forms of emotional expression, and they became "racket" or sham feelings that we used to manipulate others. Some of our families were "anger" families or "sadness" families or "guilt" families. Although adult racket feelings can appear dramatic because we are good at them, they do not advance recovery or help us achieve what we need in relationships. "Anger" people are good at blaming others; "sadness" people are good at being hurt and helpless, and "guilt" people blame themselves and apologize all the time.

Racket feelings backfire on us in adult relationships. In most cases, "anger" people are really feeling hurt, ashamed and afraid. When they express racket anger, other people pull away, and they end up feeling more afraid and hurt. "Sadness" people often feel mistreated and angry, but when they express racket sadness other people may be turned off and mistreat them more. "Guilt" people often want acceptance and love, but when they express racket guilt people may reject them and consider them "wimps." Racket feelings become just another form of compulsive behavior. We need to know what our "racket programming" is and begin to practice expressing real feelings. We usually know when we encounter someone else's racket feelings; in fact, compassionate group treatment is helpful during recovery because people can point out to us when they see us using racket emotions.

Our task, once we get beyond racket feelings, is to tell our story on a real emotional level to people who care. We need to lose ourselves in childhood feelings, in safe settings, so that we can go on with our lives unencumbered by pain. As we recover, we realize that we got stuck at some point along the path of normal development and have a hurt, frightened or angry little boy or girl hiding behind our adult facade. We must revisit those painful experiences of childhood or earlier adulthood, feel our discounted feelings and bring those hurts and traumas to new, functional endings. New behavioral and emotional freedom opens up to us as a result, and we look and feel like different people.

Facing Abandonment

Deanna asked her therapy group to help her with her angry feelings about a violent incident in her stepfamily when she was eight. She began to describe the dramatic family scene, but members of the group were restless. Several people pointed out to Deanna that they were not observing real feeling. Deanna had unconsciously chosen to talk about something that seemed impressive but actually had no emotional connection for her. Deanna felt ashamed after this feedback, but she was encouraged to try to remember a time in her past when she felt that she could not be herself. After a few moments, she remembered that when her mother died (when Deanna was three), she was sent for a time to live with relatives who resented her. She asked a woman from the group to role-play her mother for a few moments so that she could say good-bye. Everyone in the group cried as the abandoned little girl sobbed in her mother's arms. By the end of the evening, Deanna, who had appeared very young for her 34 years, seemed older and radiated a new calm and confidence.

Reenactment Of Traumatic Events

One reason for treatment failures in the past was that purely verbal approaches were used for people who had experienced extreme trauma. Just talking about what happened was not enough for many of us who grew up in troubled families. Experiences that involved terror, rage, abandonment, invasion, extreme humiliation, deprivation or abuse sometimes can be resolved only through psychodramatic reenactment. We need to role-play the traumatic scenes when we are ready, bringing with us our adult power and the support of a loving group. In that context, we can experience again exactly what it was like for us then, release rage, comfort our terrified or abandoned child-selves and rescue them forever from the scenes that haunt them.

Release Of Hatred

As a boy, Ben had been nearly fatally beaten by his mother. In his adult life, he emotionally punished some of the women he dated. He felt great remorse after he rejected or said mean things to his lovers, but he hadn't been able to stop the pattern. In a psychodrama group, Ben re-created the scene in which his mother had lost control and beaten him until he was uncon-

scious after he had broken a window in a neighbor's house.
When Ben was beaten in his group (harmlessly, of course), he
remembered his terror and hatred. He released his terrible
rage at his mother by beating on pillows, shouting, crying and
cursing until his anger was completely spent. Then Ben held a
fantasy conversation with his mother, who was now dead, and
for the first time was able to see within her the overwhelmed
little girl who was herself violently abused as a child. With his
anger and hurt behind him, Ben's heart softened and he could
forgive her at last. In his later relationships, Ben had to self-
consciously practice loving behavior with women, but this
past trauma no longer indirectly controlled his life.

Dealing With Our Families During Recovery

Many of us seek help individually, either before or after
other members of our families of childhood or adulthood get
help for themselves. Some members of our families never
become involved in recovery, while all members of other
families seek help, attend self-help groups and take part in
family therapy to heal together. There is seldom a perfect
match of various family members' needs, feelings and
behavior. For adult children, recovery may involve being
apart for a time from families that do not understand or
support our efforts. It can be threatening to parents and
siblings that family secrets are being shared, and family
members may fear that the stories told about them are
distorted and unfair (which they may be). Recovering parents
find it hard to see that their children are still wounded and
floundering while they pursue recovery themselves (Wegscheider-Cruse, 1985).

When any member of a family system begins to explore
him- or herself and grow, the system changes. The tremendous power of recovery is that when we stop trying to coerce
or influence other family members and focus on ourselves,
they begin to change. The timetable may not be to our liking,
but the changes happen nonetheless. Only after we have
achieved substantial recovery for ourselves can we seriously
consider trying to help the people we love, who may be
destroying themselves. Acting too soon to help can become a
familiar and destructive replay of our old expectations of

other family members. When we arrive at forgiveness and love, we can hope to have an impact, but to achieve these we usually have to face our own grief first.

William Worden describes four tasks of grief (1982):

1. To accept the reality of the loss
2. To experience the pain of grief
3. To adjust to an environment in which what is lost is missing
4. To withdraw emotional energy and reinvest it elsewhere

These tasks apply specifically to grieving a death, but they also pertain to the grief we feel, whether other family members are living or dead, that our families were not the way we needed them to be. We examine the reality of our losses, seeing clearly and compassionately how things went right or wrong as we grew up. As we recognize what the costs have been to ourselves and to those we love, we experience the pain of our grief. We adjust to our loss by adding to our lives, people and resources that can give us back some of what we missed. In adulthood, we naturally begin to withdraw emotional energy from our families of childhood and invest it in our love relationships, careers, friends and our own children. If we become parents, we find out how many ways there are for a parent to go wrong, and our compassion for our own parents steadily increases. We become ready to forgive.

There are certain prerequisites for forgiveness:

1. Grieving the loss and recognizing both our pain and anger
2. Taking responsibility for our own part (if any) in what happened
3. Discovering that we can go on with our lives
4. Recognizing the mitigating factors (if any) that explain other peoples' behavior
5. Understanding that our own lack of forgiveness wounds us
6. Realizing that we also need forgiveness

By the time we emotionally understand these steps, we often go beyond forgiveness and arrive at gratitude. As our hurt and anger fade, we remember and appreciate the good things. As we learn more about our parents' childhoods and

lives, we usually see that they gave us more than they
received. We can't help but love them. However wounded we
were, we made it through.

Beginning To Trust

We often lived in perpetual states of fear and insecurity as
children. As we take steps to recover, we overcome our distrust
of ourselves, others and the world. We self-consciously decide
to risk therapy or support groups because our own efforts to
solve our problems have failed. We have to find out if there
might be a better way. As children, not trusting was a way of
protecting ourselves from greater emotional losses than we
could sustain. Our conclusions that other family members and
our environments were unpredictable or untrustworthy were
often accurate. Further wounding might have put us in
emotionally impossible positions, so that we began to behave in
the world as we do when we are physically injured: constantly
aware of our vulnerability and compensating in our actions to
avoid further pain or damage. Emotionally, this often meant
we didn't let anyone get too close, didn't share ourselves
because of fear of rejection or rejected others at the first sign of
conflict or difference so that we would not be abandoned.

As we heal from our hurts of the past, we become less
preoccupied about the possibility of future hurts. We regain
the capacity to emotionally confront the painful events that
may lie ahead for us. Through recovery, we regain our
capacity to take risks.

We will have moments when we fear that we won't continue
to grow and learn. We become afraid that things are going too
well, and our old defenses come into play. We are tempted to
pull the roof in on ourselves so that we won't be taken by
surprise when disaster strikes. Our compulsive escapes may
beckon us, and we may become tantalized by the possibility
of throwing away the recovery gains we have achieved. In
order to avoid making destructive choices, we must carry out
the daily recovery activities that we know we need. When
moments of trial overtake us, we draw on this "spiritual bank
account" to help us make sane choices.

We couldn't trust our own feelings as children because we
lacked power to act, but now we have access to adult

information and skills for facing life. Self-help groups give us the opportunity to observe people with resources equal to ours confronting, struggling through and overcoming all sorts of life problems. We may feel grateful that we do not have to walk in their shoes, but we see with our own eyes that it is possible to maintain recovery in the face of anything — death of a spouse, terminal illness, troubled children, divorce, death or illness of a child, bankruptcy, imprisonment or unemployment. There is a recovery saying, "I was always complaining about the ruts in the road until I realized that the ruts are the road." As we overcome our survival patterns, we find that we can master setbacks in life that would formerly have sapped our energy and joy.

Image 13 portrays this mastery (p. 124).

Continuation Of Recovery

Unlike a biological child, who is under our care for only a brief time, the child within us is under our care for life. We can risk the possibility of new hurts that come along in life, but our inner child's tolerance for exposure to abuse, insanity and deprivation is gone forever. *We have to protect ourselves.* We have to use our adult power, discrimination and information to find trustworthy people and environments in which we can become the best possible versions of ourselves as fully functioning adults.

All of our relationships operate within explicit or implicit *contracts* about how things will be between us and the other people in our lives. For instance, in our relationship or marriage contracts, there is usually an implicit or explicit understanding that both people will be sexually faithful. Our contracts help us meet our needs in our relationship with our family of childhood, in our love relationships and at work. (These needs were identified in the "Personal Process Inventory" in Chapter 10.) Some of our needs are nonnegotiable. For instance, protection from abuse, insanity or deprivation are nonnegotiable because we cannot maintain recovery if we are exposed to them.

In the past, we often made contracts on the basis of illusions, and the result was disastrous. Some of the illusions behind our contracts were: (1) "Things will change for the better," (2) "I can succeed where others have failed," (3) "I can get used to it," (4) "I can find a relationship or job situation in which I will

Dancing through the Rattlesnakes. *This cowgirl is the master of her environment, gracefully skirting the rattlesnakes that surround her.*

be taken care of and then relax," and (5) "If I don't act on this opportunity I will never have another chance."

In light of adult reality, we revise these to: (1) "I can change myself for the better, but other people do not reliably change because I want them to," (2) "I can succeed where others have failed if I have the resources and strength to do what needs to be done and if my goal is not dependent on the actions of others who are not committed to the same end," (3) "I will not recover a tolerance for things in life that I have been chronically exposed to as a child or earlier in adult life," (4) "If I choose to let myself be taken care of, I become a victim when my needs diverge from those of the person or organization that is caring for me," and (5) "If I feel compelled to act on a certain opportunity, it is often a sign that I am overlooking some problem in myself or in the situation."

Peter Ossorio (1976) suggests developing a personal "entrance exam" for all your close personal or work relationships. You can specify your own contract requirements to use as a valuable tool for checking your decisions.

Your Entrance Exam

Based on your past experience with people and job situations, what are the nonnegotiable requirements (distinct from preferences) you need to maintain in close personal or work relationships for the sake of your health and well-being? List characteristics you: (1) must have and (2) can't stand.

Some Sample Requirements
Must Have:
1. People who basically like and respect me
2. Relationships in which conflicts can be resolved
3. A respect for people and spiritual concern for life
4. Honesty and reliability
5. A sense of humor

Can't Stand:
1. People who are not making efforts to recover from their own survival behavior and emotional patterns
2. People who habitually mistreat others
3. Ruthless ambition
4. Covert hostility
5. People who are actively using compulsive escapes

Using Your Entrance Exam

Once you have your entrance requirements, you are in a position to evaluate the information you have about people and job situations before you enter into new contracts. People will generally let you know directly or indirectly what you can expect from them during the initial stages of interaction, but you have to use your eyes, ears and intuition. As you evaluate a relationship or job situation, pay attention to what is said and not said, what you can learn about the history of the situation or person, and how you feel during and after the interaction. Ask questions to get the information you need. Check the information you get against your nonnegotiable requirements, and, if necessary, discuss any questions that remain ambiguous to you with someone you can trust. If your requirements are met, you can feel free to proceed with the next stage of commitment to the person or situation. Your entrance exam is your implicit contract. If your requirements are not met, hold out for what you know you need, but be prepared to say goodbye in a respectful manner if you cannot achieve this.

If you are currently in a situation in which your entrance requirements are not met, be aware that you cannot remain there for long without harming yourself. Do what is possible to negotiate for what you need, and if you cannot achieve this, find a healthier situation for yourself.

Give Yourself The Life You Want

A friend once asked, "How many days do you have left?" We don't know how many days of life we have left, but we can be sure that it is not an infinite number. Through all of our recovery efforts, we have gained the freedom to make choices, to put the pain of the past behind us, to see things as they are and to be unfettered by compulsive behavior. Our task for each of our remaining days is to live that day as if it were our last. In this way we build lives we can enjoy and be proud of.

As you go on with your life, write down your vision of a perfect day one year from now, five years from now and fifteen years from now. Develop a written plan about how you want to live today and what you need to do in preparation for those perfect days ahead. Enjoy your journey!

REFERENCES

Alcoholics Anonymous. (3rd ed.). New York: Alcoholics Anonymous World Services, 1976.

Black, Claudia. **It Will Never Happen To Me.** Denver: M.A.C. Printing and Publications, 1981.

Bowen, Murray. "Theory in the Practice of Family Therapy" in Guerin, Phillip J. (ed.). **Family Therapy: Theory and Practice.** New York: Gardner Press, 1976.

Burns, David D. **Feeling Good: The New Mood Therapy.** New York: The New American Library, 1980.

Carnes, Patrick. **The Sexual Addiction.** Minneapolis: CompCare Publications, 1983.

Cruse, Joseph. *The Romance.* Speech given at Family Reconstruction Workshop, Palm Springs, CA, June, 1984.

Curran, Dolores. **Traits Of A Healthy Family.** New York: Ballantine Books, 1983.

Goulding, Mary M., and Goulding, Robert L. **Changing Lives Through Redecision Therapy.** New York: Brunner/Mazel, 1979.

Greenleaf, Jael. *Co-Alcoholic-Para-Alcoholic: Who's Who And What's The Difference?* Paper presented at the National Council on Alcoholism, 1981 Annual Alcoholism Forum, New Orleans, April 12, 1981.

Johnson, Vernon. **I'll Quit Tomorrow.** New York: Harper & Row, 1973.

Kaufman, Gershen. **Shame: The Power Of Caring.** Cambridge, MA: Schenkman, 1980.

Kiley, Dan. **The Peter Pan Syndrome: Men Who Have Never Grown Up.** New York: Dodd, Mead, 1983.

Lasater, Lane. "Stress and Health in a Colorado Coal Mining Community" in Davis, K.E., and Bergner, R.E. **Advances In**

Descriptive Psychology. vol. 3, Greenwich, CT: JAI Press, 1983.

Lerner, Rokelle. **Daily Affirmations For Adult Children Of Alcoholics.** Pompano Beach, FL: Health Communications, 1985.

Maslow, Abraham H. 1943. "A Theory of Human Motivation." *Psychol. Rev.* **50.**

Milkman, Harvey, and Sunderwirth, Stanley. 1982. "Addictive Processes." *Psychoactive Drugs* **14,** no. 3.

Miller, Alice. **Thou Shalt Not Be Aware: Society's Betrayal Of The Child.** New York: Farrar, Straus, Giroux, 1984.

Norwood, Robin. **Women Who Love Too Much.** Los Angeles: Jeremy P. Tarcher, 1985.

Ossorio, Peter G. *Clinical Topics: A Seminar In Descriptive Psychology.* L.R.I. Report No. 11. Whittier, CA, and Boulder, CO: Linguistic Research Institute, 1976.

Ossorio, Peter G. *Positive Health and Transcendental Theories: A Seminar In Descriptive Psychology.* L.R.I. Report No. 13. Whittier, CA, and Boulder, CO: Linguistic Research Institute, 1977.

Schiff, Jacqui L. et al. **The Cathexis Reader: The Transactional Analysis Treatment Of Psychosis.** New York: Harper & Row, 1975.

Wegscheider, Sharon. **Another Chance: Hope And Help For The Alcoholic Family.** Palo Alto, CA: Science and Behavior Books, 1981.

Wegscheider-Cruse, Sharon. **Choice-Making: For Co-Dependents, Adult Children And Spirituality Seekers.** Pompano Beach, FL: Health Communications, 1985.

Whitfield, Charles L. **Healing The Child Within: Discovery And Recovery For Adult Children Of Dysfunctional Families.** Pompano Beach, FL: Health Communications, 1987.

Woolams, Stan, and Brown, Michael. **The Total Handbook Of Transactional Analysis.** Englewood Cliffs, NJ: Prentice Hall, 1979.

Worden, J. William. **Grief Counseling And Grief Therapy: A Handbook For The Mental Health Practitioner.** New York: Springer Publishing, 1982.

ABOUT THE AUTHOR

Lane Lasater is a clinical psychologist who specializes in helping individuals, couples and families overcome compulsive patterns. He works with people who live in or grew up in troubled families. Dr. Lasater directs the Colorado Renewal Center in Boulder, Colorado, presents workshops for people from troubled families, trains and supervises psychotherapists who work in that area and serves as a consultant to alcohol treatment centers in Colorado. He received a bachelor's degree from Princeton University, a master's degree from Ohio State University and master's degree and Ph.D. from the University of Colorado at Boulder. He continued training in child, adolescent and family psychology at the University of Minnesota Health Sciences Center in Minneapolis, before returning to Colorado. He lives in Boulder with his wife Nancy and their children, Colin and Jonathan. Dr. Lasater can be reached at Colorado Renewal Center, Suite 102, 5353 Manhattan Circle, Boulder, Colorado, 80303; Telephone (303) 494-2565.

Other Books By . . .

HEALTH COMMUNICATIONS, INC.

Enterprise Center
3201 Southwest 15th Street
Deerfield Beach, FL 33442
Phone: 800-851-9100

ADULT CHILDREN OF ALCOHOLICS
Janet Woititz
Over a year on The New York Times Best Seller list,this book is the primer
on Adult Children of Alcoholics.
ISBN 0-932194-15-X $6.95

STRUGGLE FOR INTIMACY
Janet Woititz
Another best seller, this book gives insightful advice on learning to love
more fully.
ISBN 0-932194-25-7 $6.95

DAILY AFFIRMATIONS: For Adult Children of Alcoholics
Rokelle Lerner
These positive affirmations for every day of the year paint a mental picture
of your life as you choose it to be.
ISBN 0-932194-27-3 $6.95

*CHOICEMAKING: For Co-dependents, Adult Children and Spirituality
Seekers* — Sharon Wegscheider-Cruse
This useful book defines the problems and solves them in a positive way.
ISBN 0-932194-26-5 $9.95

LEARNING TO LOVE YOURSELF: Finding Your Self-Worth
Sharon Wegscheider-Cruse
"Self-worth is a choice, not a birthright", says the author as she shows us
how we can choose positive self-esteem.
ISBN 0-932194-39-7 $7.95

LET GO AND GROW: Recovery for Adult Children
Robert Ackerman
An in-depth study of the different characteristics of adult children of
alcoholics with guidelines for recovery.
ISBN 0-932194-51-6 $8.95

LOST IN THE SHUFFLE: The Co-dependent Reality
Robert Subby
A look at the unreal rules the co-dependent lives by and the way out of the
dis-eased reality.
ISBN 0-932194-45-1 $8.95

Books from . . .
Health Communications

THIRTY-TWO ELEPHANT REMINDERS: A Book of Healthy Rules
Mary M. McKee
Concise advice by 32 wise elephants whose wit and good humor will also
be appearing in a 12-step calendar and greeting cards.
ISBN 0-932194-59-1 $3.95

BREAKING THE CYCLE OF ADDICTION: For Adult Children of Alcoholics
Patricia O'Gorman and Philip Oliver-Diaz
For parents who were raised in addicted families, this guide teaches you
about Breaking the Cycle of Addiction from *your* parents to your children.
Must reading for any parent.
ISBN 0-932194-37-0 $8.95

AFTER THE TEARS: Reclaiming The Personal Losses of Childhood
Jane Middelton-Moz and Lorie Dwinnel
Your lost childhood must be grieved in order for you to recapture your
self-worth and enjoyment of life. This book will show you how.
ISBN 0-932194-36-2 $7.95

ADULT CHILDREN OF ALCOHOLICS SYNDROME: From Discovery to Recovery
Wayne Kritsberg
Through the Family Integration System and foundations for healing the
wounds of an alcoholic-influenced childhood are laid in this important
book.
ISBN 0-932194-30-3 $7.95

OTHERWISE PERFECT: People and Their Problems with Weight
Mary S. Stuart and Lynnzy Orr
This book deals with all the varieties of eating disorders, from anorexia to
obesity, and how to cope sensibly and successfully.
ISBN 0-932194-57-5 $7.95

Orders must be prepaid by check, money order, MasterCard or Visa.
Purchase orders from agencies accepted (attach P.O. documentation)
for billing. Net 30 days.
    Minimum shipping/handling — $1.25 for orders less than $25. For
orders over $25, add 5% of total for shipping and handling. Florida
residents add 5% sales tax.